About the Cover

"Shooter's Odds"
A painting by Ross Buckland

Captain Ralph Parr narrowly escaped death after rolling his aircraft into a Split-S forcing his F-86F straight down from 41,000 feet and closed rapidly on the suspicious image. Soon, he saw four MiG-15s in front of him, but a quick look left and right revealed that there was really a total of 16 enemy aircraft. Not one to miss an opportunity, Parr engaged the closest aircraft and was immediately in a boiling dogfight right on the deck. Note the speed breaks deployed on lower aft fuselage and the red stripe on Ralph's helmet seen in the cockpit.

Photo by Leslie Plaza Johnson

Ken Murray was born and raised in Hudson, Iowa. He was an understudy in the publishing business as his parents owned and operated Hudson Printing Company for more than 49 years, until his father's passing in 2011. He worked his way through high school and college in the family business and graduated with a bachelor's degree in public relations/journalism minor from the University of Northern Iowa in 1985.

He joined the Air Force in 1986 and earned his MBA in 1990 from the University of South Dakota. He was an instructor/evaluator navigator on KC-135 air refueling tankers and also spent many years as an instructor navigator at the Nav School at Randolph AFB, TX. Murray is a combat veteran who flew missions in support of Operations Just Cause, Desert Storm, Allied Force, and was chief of combat operations at the Combined Air Operations Center at Al Udeid AB, Qatar, supporting Iraqi Freedom and Enduring Freedom.

He also served as editor of Torch Magazine, Air Education and Training Command's Safety Magazine, where his team won the International Blue Pencil Award for government communicators. A highly decorated Air Force officer, Murray retired from the Air Force on 1 May 2011, as a Lt. Colonel after a 25-year career.

Dedication

Cliff Murray mentored me as a young boy, working my way through middle school, high school, and college in the family printing business. He taught me how to run a linotype in the days of hot type until the company's conversion to electronic typesetting in the early '80s and the offset-printing process.

My post-air force plan was to write his biography with him during my retirement. That plan was dashed when he passed away on May 2, 2011, the day after I retired. It's only fitting that this work, a book detailing the illustrious life of my other hero, Colonel Ralph Parr, be dedicated to my dad's memory—he taught me everything I know about the publishing business. Dad, this one's for you.

Ken Murray

ON PARR

THE STUNNING COMBAT MISSIONS OF AMERICAN FIGHTER ACE, COLONEL RALPH PARR

AUSTIN MACAULEY PUBLISHERS™

LONDON · CAMBRIDGE · NEW YORK · SHARJAH

A CIP catalogue record for this title is available from the British Library.

ISBN 9781786939166 (Paperback)
ISBN 9781786939173 (Hardback)
ISBN 9781786939180 (E-Book)

www.austinmacauley.com

First Published (2018)
Austin Macauley Publishers Ltd™
25 Canada Square
Canary Wharf
London
E14 5LQ

Acknowledgments

Dr. Rebecca L. Murray
Ms. Margie Wetenkamp-Castle, Editor
Ms. Lynnette Gonzales, Editor
Mr. Ed Pickrel, Colonel, USAF (Ret.)
Mr. Wayne Mudge, Colonel, USAF (Ret.)
Air Force Historical Research Agency (AFHRA)

Table of Contents

A Note to Readers   19

Preface   20

Chapter 1   23

Napalm Delivery   23

Chapter 2   44

44 Years Earlier   44

Chapter 3   53

Sunday Surprise   53

Chapter 4   71

Young Guns   71

Chapter 5   92

Tank Busting   92

Chapter 6   103

Can I Run Any Faster?   103

Chapter 7   110

F-86s in Korea   110

Chapter 8   **131**

Dirty Guns   *131*

Chapter 9   **147**

Against All Odds   *147*

Chapter 10   **163**

When Last Was First   *163*

Chapter 11   **191**

Vietnam   *191*

Chapter 12   **215**

Risky Iran   *215*

Chapter 13   **223**

Unsuspecting Fall Finale   *223*

Chapter 14   **233**

Eight Years Earlier—Re-attack   *233*

Chapter 15   **244**

Short String   *244*

Chapter 16   **264**

Ralph Parr, A Stick and Rudder Artist   **267**

A Historic Man   **270**

APPENDIX I   **271**

    Awards and Citations   *271*

APPENDIX II   **302**

    Education and Service   *302*

APPENDIX III   **312**

    Decorations and Service Awards   *312*

Bibliography   **314**

Index   **321**

"Every fighter pilot likes to believe that he or she is the 'World's Greatest Fighter Pilot' but only a few truly are in the running for that honor—Rickenbacker, Von Richthofen, Bong, Hartmann, McConnell, and Olds to name a few. Ralph Parr easily falls into this grouping. His willingness to attack, regardless of the odds and danger involved, set a standard for all to strive to and a legacy to honor. A Warrior's Warrior! A life story that every pilot needs to know."

William R. Looney III, General, USAF (Ret.)

"Ralph Parr is an American hero in every sense of the word and Ken Murray has captured the essence of what being a hero is all about. Parr was the epitome of a fighter pilot, exemplifying the attributes of integrity, excellence, and service before self. It's rare to find such an honest and candid accounting of life lessons told through heart-wrenching war stories in such an understandable way. I couldn't put it down until it was finished—a book for the ages."

Dave Deptula, Lieutenant General, USAF (Ret.)
Dean, The Mitchell Institute for Aerospace Studies

"Ralph Parr set a mark of devotion to duty, courage, and airmanship in three wars that no other pilot in the U.S. Air Force has matched."

Charles G. (Chick) Cleveland, Lieutenant General, USAF (Ret.)
President, American Fighter Aces Association

"Ken Murray's first-hand account of Ralph Parr's aerial encounters is so realistic that the only thing you, the reader, lack is sweat from under a helmet draining into your eyes, your oxygen mask cutting into your cheeks and the hard knot of an inflated G-suit in your gut. If you want to experience air combat, read *On Parr*!"

Chuck Horner, General, USAF (Ret.)
Air Boss Desert Storm

"This is the story of a great friend and a fighter pilot whose abilities knew no limits. He flew P-38s in WWII, F-80s and F-86s in Korea and the F-4 in Vietnam. In Korea, flying the F-86, he became a Double Jet Ace and one of the three pilots, all of whom are the leading living USAF Jet Aces. Ralph Parr has been decorated more than 60 times and is the only USAF fighter pilot to earn the Distinguished Service Cross and the Air Force Cross. When you read *On Parr*, you'll be reading of a man whose primary mission, as he applied power for takeoff, was duty, honor, and country."

Frederick 'Boots' Blesse, Maj. Gen., USAF (Ret.)
Korean War Double Ace; Author, 'No Guts No Glory'
Author's Note: Boots' endorsement was written before he and Ralph passed away.

"Col. Ralph Parr—hero, mentor, leader. An impressive fighter pilot, he has done it all. When I first met Ralph and saw all of his medals, I knew that I was in the presence of a great warrior. Five combat tours in three wars and 641 combat missions. Mission accomplishment was always important, especially when it supported troops on the ground. In addition, he was always quite a gentleman. I am extremely glad to have had him as a friend."

Col. Chuck Debellevue, Colonel, USAF (Ret.)
Vietnam Ace—credited with six kills

Flying Ace or **Fighter Ace** is a military aviator credited with shooting down several enemy aircraft during aerial combat. The actual number of aerial victories required to officially qualify as an 'ace' has varied but is usually considered to be five or more. The few aces among combat pilots have historically accounted for the majority of air-to-air victories in military history.

A Note to Readers

I spent more than two years interviewing and gathering research for this work and was granted unlimited access to Ralph Parr and his family. We lost Ralph in 2012, and while my notes on his life are copious, they're never enough when writing about heroism and skill as a fighter pilot. With that in mind, I've taken certain literary liberties along the way, to give Ralph's story the narrative flow it deserves. For example, we don't know exactly how fast Ralph's F-86 was traveling when he frantically pulled out of a 9.5G dive from 41,000 feet, so I filled the gaps with a 'best guess' based on technical data and discussions with other pilots from that era, who would know.

Much of the book is written directly from Ralph's words, and while some incidental details may be contrived, I can assure you that the technical aviation and combat details are accurate. The story longs for personal photos and letters from the past; however, Ralph and Margaret lost nearly everything during a horrific flood in 1998.

Ken Murray
December 2017

Preface

This book's message is one of inspiration. It's one man's gut-wrenching stories of conquering extraordinary odds on countless occasions. Through a myriad of near-death experiences that would make the average man recoil, Colonel Ralph S. Parr, a steely-eyed fighter pilot of old, emerges from the omnipresent danger, ubiquitous risk and persistent threats as a true American hero, dominant of all but time and cancer.

He details war stories from World War II, Korean and Vietnam Wars as if they occurred yesterday. A Korean War Double Ace, he retained many fighter-pilot traits as he told dog-fighting stories, using his hands to illustrate his relative position on a feisty MiG-15 in MiG Alley. He rarely suffered from fear of the unknown but was duly accountable for the butterflies present in the guts of enemy fighter pilots, who dared to fight 'that guy' with the red stripe.

His stories undulate from one end of the emotional spectrum to the other. In some cases, a lopsided smile creeps across his face as he reminisces. Then, the story steers on a different vector, filling his eyes with tears. Col. Parr reveals his unyielding passion for flight, freedom, and patriotism, culminating an illustrious 34-year air force career as he describes his matchless achievements earning him more than 60 decorations. He's the only man in history to earn the Distinguished Service Cross and the Air Force Cross.

You will undoubtedly put this book down, feeling rejuvenated, motivated, and holding a belief that you can accomplish anything, regardless of the odds. You, too, will be inspired and *ON PARR* once you're acquainted with this patriot and true American hero.

Colonel Ralph S. Parr
U. S. Air Force, Retired

Ralph Sherman Parr is a jet fighter ace whose unique combination of flying ability, significant achievement, and heroic service span three wars and five combat tours. Colonel Parr is a Command Pilot with over 8,000 flying hours in more than 8 different fighter aircraft. He began his fighter career in the P-38 during WWII, then flew the P-51 and F-84 until he was assigned to Korea in 1950, flying the F-80. He flew another tour in Korea in 1953, where he scored 10 victories against enemy aircraft, and was awarded the Distinguished Service Cross for extraordinary heroism. After Korea, Col Parr served in a number of staff and operational assignments, including playing a leadership role in bringing the F-4C Phantom to operational status in the USAF in 1963. Assigned to Cam Ranh Bay, Republic of Vietnam in 1967, as Wing DO, Col Parr flew 226 combat missions in the F-4C Phantom II, receiving the Air Force Cross for a critical mission during the battle for Khe Sanh. Col Parr flew a second tour in Vietnam as wing Commander of the 12th TFW, where he flew an additional 201 combat missions. Col Parr retired in 1976, and holds the greatest number of awards and decorations of any living Air Force Officer.

This plaque summarizes Colonel Ralph S. Parr's achievements during his 34-year air force career and was displayed on the wall of his room until the day he passed away.

Chapter 1
Napalm Delivery

Today's headline back home was '*RFK still not in political race*' with the ensuing story highlighting the political upheaval in America while forecasting the election landscape for November. The story read: *Sen. Robert F. Kennedy weighed grassroots encouragement against rising party opposition today, as he sought to make up his mind whether to challenge Lyndon B. Johnson and Sen. Eugene J. McCarthy for the democratic presidential nomination.*

The New York Senator's Capitol Hill office buzzed Thursday with phone calls, telegrams, special-delivery letters, and visitors, who urged him to resolve his 'reassessment' of the presidential race by declaring his candidacy.[1]

It was Saturday, March 16, 1968, and a half world away, the highly politicized war in Vietnam raged on. The Siege of Khe Sanh, a U.S. Marine base in South Vietnam, was well under way and Ralph S. Parr, a 44-year-old USAF Colonel and seasoned fighter pilot, was the commander of the 12th Operations Group at Cam Ranh Bay.

---

[1] (RFK still not in political race)

A product of the Cold War, the Southeast Asia War (1961-1973) began with communist attempts to overthrow non-communist governments in the region. United States' participation in the Southeast Asia War resulted from the policy of 'containment', which aimed to prevent communism from expanding beyond its early Cold War borders. The containment strategy seldom led to major combat, but as with the Korean War (1950-1953), the U.S. committed large military forces to protect an allied, non-communist government.[2]

---

[2] (The Southeast Asia War: Vietnam, Laos and Cambodia)

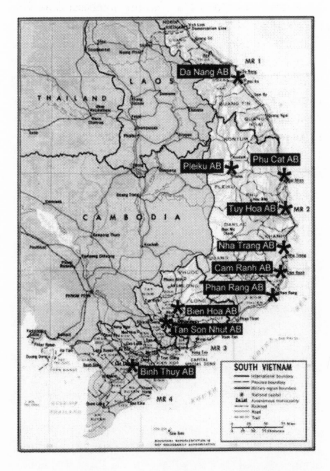

SOUTH VIETNAM

Ralph's group flew the F-4C Phantom II. First flown in May 1958, the Phantom II was originally developed for U.S. Navy fleet defense. The U.S. Air Force's first version, the F-4C, made its first flight in May 1963; production deliveries began six months later. Phantom II's production ended in 1979, after over 5,000 had been built—more than 2,600 for the USAF, about 1,200 for the United States Navy and Marine Corps, and the rest for friendly foreign nations.

In 1965, the USAF sent its first F-4Cs to Southeast Asia, where they flew air-to-air missions against North Vietnamese fighters as well as attacking ground targets. The first USAF pilot to score four combat victories with F-4s in Southeast Asia was Colonel Robin Olds, a World War II Ace.

In its air-to-ground role, the F-4C could carry twice the normal load of a WWII B-17.[3]

F-4C

Built by McDonnell Douglas, the gas-guzzling twin-engine jet fighter carried a crew of one pilot and a weapon systems officer (WSO, pronounced 'Wizzo' also 'GIB' or guy in back), and was capable of unleashing enormous firepower and ear-piercing noise produced by the two after burning J-79 engines. A shortage of WSOs in theatre forced, in many instances, a second pilot (GIB)

[3] (McDonnell Douglas F-4C Phantom II)

to occupy the back seat in order to fill the cockpits for missions each day. Ralph was as proficient as he was going to get dropping canisters of napalm and firing its deadly external gun. Life was good.

An F-4C from the 12ᵗʰ Tactical Fighter Wing drops a canister of napalm on NVA forces with devastating effects.

Ralph awoke shortly after 6 a.m. to slightly overcast skies. Overall, the weather was decent, but there was something lingering in the humid morning air. Nothing you could feel or hear or see, but you knew that it was there, silently waiting and watching for just the right moment to get your attention and not in a nice way. He was now into his morning routine in preparation for the upcoming mission that day.

Early in 1968, Khe Sanh became the focal point of enemy activity in I Corps. All evidence pointed to a North Vietnamese offensive, similar to the one in 1967, only on a much larger scale. Various intelligence sources indicated that North Vietnamese units, which usually came down and skirted the combat base, outside of artillery range, were moving into the Khe Sanh area to stay. At first, the reports showed an influx of individual regiments but then of a division. The establishment of a front headquarters indicated that at least two North Vietnamese divisions were in the vicinity.[4]

The start of the Siege of Khe Sanh began just after midnight on 21 January 1968, when Hill 861 was partially overrun. The artillery and rocket attacks (no ground troops) began at first light.[5] The North Vietnamese Army forces hammered the Khe Sanh Marine Combat Base with rockets, mortars, artillery, small arms, and automatic weapons fire. Hundreds of 82-mm mortar rounds and 122-mm rockets slammed into the combat base. Virtually all of the base's ammunition stock and a substantial portion of the fuel supplies were destroyed. The actions around Khe Sanh Combat Base, when flashed to the world, touched off a political and public uproar as to whether or not the position should be held.[6]

This buildup around Khe Sanh drastically altered the security picture at the base. The road over which the base received its supplies had been cut since August 1967. Enemy activity intensified, and because of increased use of anti-aircraft fire, it was no longer possible for U.S. forces to airlift supplies with immunity. The bulk of the

---

[4] (Pearson) 29

[5] (Mannion)

[6] (Pearson) 32-34

135 tons of supplies required daily had to be parachute to the marine and South Vietnamese forces defending the base.

The main enemy forces in the area were identified as the 325C North Vietnamese Army Division, which had moved back into the region north of Hill 881 North, and a newcomer, the 304th North Vietnamese Division, which had crossed over from Laos and established positions southwest of the base. The 304th, an elite home-guard division from Hanoi, had been a participant at Dien Bien Phu. In addition, one regiment of the 324th North Vietnamese Division was located in the central demilitarized area, some 10 to 15 miles from Khe Sanh, fulfilling a supply role.

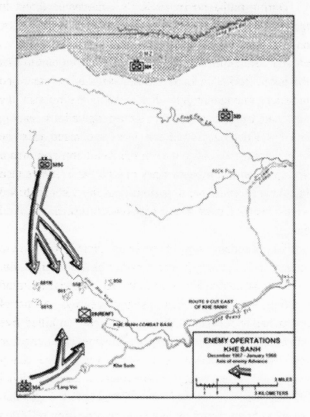

In the early stages of the siege of Khe Sanh, the presence of the 320th Division was confirmed north of the Rock Pile, within easy reinforcing distance of the enemy Khe Sanh forces. The 304th and 325C Divisions were known to have armored units with them and were supported by the North Vietnamese 68th and 164th Artillery Regiments.[7]

---

[7] (Pearson) 29-30

During mid-January 1968, the undeniable threat in the Khe Sanh area prompted the greatest concern. Not only had the enemy positioned a large number of forces around Khe Sanh, but intelligence sources reported that Routes 92 and 9 in Laos showed signs of an increased logistical movement into that area, indicating that the area had become a pivot point for operations leading towards Khe Sanh. While it was recognized that the disposition of enemy forces in the Khe Sanh area was a very real threat to the marines at Khe Sanh, it was also seen as an undeniable opportunity to direct concentrated air strikes against known enemy positions on a sustained basis.[8]

Still another sign of reviving North Vietnamese interest in Khe Sanh appeared earlier on 2 January 1968, when a marine listening post at the combat base reported sighting six unidentified persons nearby. A patrol dispatched to investigate the unidentified men killed five when they failed to respond to a challenge. Later, the five killed were identified as a North Vietnamese Army regimental commander, his operations officer, the signal officer, and two other officers. The simple thought that these key men would undertake such a mission reflected high-level enemy interest in the base.[9]

Low visibility hindered nearly every mission Ralph flew that spring, as the Vietnamese burned off the rice crops in preparation for the next growing season. These fires produced an incredible amount of smoke, creating a constant low haze that lingered at roughly 3,000 feet. The

[8] (Pearson) 30

[9] (Pearson) 30

dense haze created a surreal phenomenon where the mountainous terrain would randomly jab through the haze and cloud deck, creating an eerie but beautiful scene from the air.

It reminded Ralph of the spires on the Golden Gate Bridge, rising above the smooth ocean of early morning fog in San Francisco. Ralph took off with three other aircraft in a four-ship formation. The mission was fragged to escort and protect cargo aircraft from enemy fighters and the unrelenting anti-aircraft ground fire coming from below. The C-130s were full of much-needed supplies and Ralph's mission was to keep them safe.

Tom McManus, a second pilot and Ralph's back-seater that day, were wrapping up the escort mission when they heard a young marine's voice crackle over the radio. The marine pilot, Captain Ronald Love, an airborne forward air controller (FAC) was pleading for air support over the radio. Capt. Love was flying what looked like an L-19 'Bird Dog' single-engine prop FAC aircraft, flying low and slow to aid in spotting and marking enemy targets with smoke so faster moving strike aircraft, like the F-4C, could roll in to destroy the target.

L-19 (O-1) Bird Dog Forward Air Controller (FAC) aircraft

The uncharacteristically anxious FAC, call sign Fingerprint 54[10], yelled over the radio, "Is there anybody up here who can help me? I've got two active mortar positions and anti-aircraft guns spotted."

That call perked Ralph's ears and sent a shiver up his spine. Ralph sensed the urgent need for help and immediately passed his call sign back to Capt. Love over the radio. The transmission went through, and the 'Bird Dog' pilot immediately snatched hold of Ralph's response and call sign. There were troops in contact (TIC), American Marines at Khe Sanh in contact with the North Vietnamese Army (NVA).

Khe Sanh and its surrounding outposts were currently supplied almost entirely by air. Marine and air force cargo aircraft made numerous daily runs to keep the base provisioned, transport replacement troops, and evacuate the wounded. The pilots had to brave both poor weather and intense enemy's anti-aircraft fire to accomplish these tasks.[11]

Recent catastrophic events were still etched in the minds of many. On 10 February, a Marine C-130, loaded with fuel containers, was laced with bullets just before touching down on the runway. The aircraft was lost, along with some of the passengers and crew. This incident caused major revisions in the offloading

---

[10] (Malayney)

[11] (Pearson) 76

procedure and highlighted an increased protection requirement.[12]

The North Vietnamese had completely surrounded the marine combat base at Khe Sanh.[13] The cargo aircraft departure procedures were risky due to the ever-rising terrain, forcing them to climb at max rate and strictly adhere to its route up the valley, dangerously near the strategically placed enemy firepower. Parr and McManus lowered the nose of their Phantom to drop down to a lower altitude in hopes of better visibility. Once below the thick cloud deck, Ralph called the FAC to inform him that they were in the general area.

They continued their descent, desperately searching for Captain Love's 'Bird Dog' as he would walk Ralph and Tom precisely onto the targets. McManus asked from the back seat if there was anything Ralph wanted him to do. He was in awe of Ralph's cool and calm demeanor as they entered the high-threat area, each unsure of the ensuing situation.[14]

Ralph said, "Tom, sit back there quietly unless I ask you to take the jet or ask you for information. It's about to get busy up here."[15]

The radio transmissions between the FAC and Ralph drastically increased in rate and intensity now. The FAC

---

[12] (Pearson) 76-77

[13] (Mannion)

[14] (McManus)

[15] Tom McManus remembered, "It was evident very early on that Ralph was a seasoned professional and I was simply his apprentice as he was a full-bird colonel in his third war and I was a young, untested captain."

guided Ralph towards the target, using nothing more than large landmarks, then smaller visual references further refining the position of the target with each transmission.

The 'walk-on' dialogue between the pilots of the two aircraft is a well-choreographed and often-practiced art. The first radio call between a forward air controller and a strike aircraft during a close air support mission is the most critical. It's like establishing a meeting point when you are trying to meet some friends in a city foreign to all. You can't say, "Let's meet at the corner," and expect to find each other. Initially, large landmarks are used to ensure that all are at the same point of reference. Radio transmissions between the FAC and fighter pilot would tend to go like this:

FAC: "Phantom 01, call contact on the intersection of Highway 1 and the Nam No River?"

Pilot: "Contact."

This simple acknowledgment by the fighter pilot confirms that he and the FAC are looking at the same point on the ground.

FAC: "Walk your eyes north along Highway 1 until you see a large rock formation on the east side of the road. Call contact on that rock formation."

Pilot: "Contact."

Now, the FAC would normally confirm the formation by asking a definitive-type question.

FAC: "What color is the rock formation?"

Pilot: "The rocks look dark gray near the bottom and white on top."

FAC: "Affirm."

Now, a frame of reference for distance must be established.

FAC: "Call the distance from the intersection of Highway 1 and the river to the rock formation one unit."

At this point, the FAC and the fighter pilot have established three essential aspects of a close air-support mission: 1) A starting point of reference for visually finding a target, 2) a unit of measure to judge distance, and 3) a strong confidence in one another. Now, the FAC simply walks the pilot's eyes to the target.

FAC: "Phantom 01, from the rock formation, go one unit due east and tell me what you see."

Pilot: "I see a large rectangular-shaped field with some revetments in the northeast corner of the field."

FAC: "Phantom 01, there are four dug-in AAA pieces in those revetments. Those are your targets! You are cleared hot on those targets!"[16]

Ralph felt like he was flying blind en route to the first target, a mortar position. As the FAC walked him onto the target, Ralph rolled his F-4 in, knowing that he had to attack as quickly as possible, cherishing the element of surprise. Their F-4C, tail #640726, was loaded out with four canisters of napalm and 1150 rounds of 20-mm ammo available in the external (pod-mounted) gun. Their wingman, F-4C tail #640679, was piloted by Major Edward D. Silver and Lt. Col. Ernest Craigwell in Silver's backseat. They carried 6 x 500lb. bombs and 1150 of 20-mm gun rounds, ready for the FAC's targets.

---

[16] (Cerone)

Colonel Parr's aircraft loaded with four canisters of napalm and external fuel tanks.
(Norman Malayney photo)

Most importantly, there were friendlies located a mere 50-75 meters northeast of the target complex, so impeccable weapons delivery accuracy was required, negating any chance of fratricide.[17]

It was 1325 hours, or 1:25 pm local, and Parr and McManus were each under the impression that the engagement would last until they were out of weapons or gas, whichever occurred first.

As Parr and McManus headed towards the target, McManus said, "This is great, we've got the sun at our back," an aspect forcing the enemy to stare directly into the sun in search of the approaching fighter while totally illuminating the hillside for Parr and McManus' target run. This simple lighting aspect would be a significant

---

[17] The friendlies' location was confirmed by an additional after-action report submitted by the FAC the following day, 17 March 1968 and was provided courtesy of the 12 TFW Assn., Historian, Norman Malaney.

advantage by vastly improving their visual acuity through the smoke and haze in the South Vietnam skies.

Their first target run was a 'dry pass' (no weapons delivery), and as Parr and McManus came across the target, they each heard the banging of the anti-aircraft guns and felt the dreaded impact of two rounds; one in each wing of their Phantom. As Ralph pulled the nose up to begin the setup for their first napalm run, McManus said, "Sir, we've been hit. We've got holes in each wing."

Parr replied, "Are you okay?"

A young and semi-startled Capt. McManus said, "I don't know, I've never been shot at."

Ralph replied, "Well, I don't know either because I've never been hit."

Once they ensured that all engine indications were normal, Parr calmly said, "Do you mind if we go back in, Tom?"

McManus replied, "Let's go."[18]

Tom was amazed at Ralph's overall bearing in the cockpit during the intense 25-minute engagement. McManus had flown with other pilots who would nearly hyperventilate during engagements, even in the training environment.[19] Ralph punched the pickle button, used to unleash a canister of napalm, from his F-4's under wing

---

[18] (McManus)

[19] McManus would remember, "I was in awe at Col. Parr's actions that day. There was no excitement, no emotion, no yelling, and no huffing and puffing. He was simply one true professional flying in the front seat and I was his apprentice."

hard point. It was a direct hit, striking the leading edge of the mortar position. A massive explosion erupted as the flaming jelly quickly spread like a kitchen grease fire. Flames and debris flew indiscriminately throughout the dug-in mortar emplacement.

Napalm (naphthenic palmitic acid) is an incendiary weapon invented in 1942. It is an extremely flammable, gasoline-based defoliant and an antipersonnel weapon that can generate temperatures in excess of 2,000 degrees.

A large napalm fire can create a wind system, a result of intense heat that is generated, causing vertical wind currents. Winds then feed more air into the fire, which increases the rate of combustion, thereby perpetuating itself. That wind is called a 'fire storm' in some cases and can reach up to 70 mph.

Cpl. Dennis Mannion, an artillery forward observer on Hill 861 during the entire Khe Sanh siege, was observing an airstrike through his binoculars one day and witnessed this phenomenon. An NVA soldier popped up from his secluded position less than 500 meters away to fire an AK-47 at an approaching fighter, totally oblivious to the napalm canister tumbling through the air towards him. The bomb's concussion and its ensuing wall of flame launched him backwards in the air for nearly 20 feet as if he'd been hit by an enormous ocean wave. He was then incinerated when the flames caught up to him.[20]

In Vietnam, the most frequently used container of napalm held about 130 gallons of gasoline, with a solution of six percent napalm added. When dropped

---

[20] (Mannion)

from 'hedge-hopping'—those flying at an altitude of about 100 feet—the device was able to cover a surface with flames 270-feet long and 75-feet wide.

Frequently, when American military forces were being over-run in Vietnam, air strikes were called in to stabilize an escalating situation with napalm and other airborne explosives. However, the North Vietnamese Army (NVA) quickly caught on to this devastating weapon and would 'dig-in', finding shelter underground in thousands of connecting tunnel systems.

In Vietnam, napalm was as much a psychological weapon as a killing weapon.[21]

The FAC couldn't contain himself. He seemed amazed and overwhelmed that Ralph hit it with such accuracy. But there was no choice. Ralph knew that pinpoint accuracy was required the first time. The Khe Sanh Base had been under siege for weeks. Mass casualties could be in the near future; there was no time for second-guessing.

That first hit was within 10 feet of the mortar itself. Ralph quickly and expertly egressed that target and kept his head cranked around, peering over his left shoulder, so as not to lose visual contact with the target area. He banked the aircraft around to set up a pattern, so he could run multiple passes over the target area as safely and quickly as possible. One main threat had been eliminated, but there were more deadly forces below that had to be eliminated.

---

[21] ("Napalm")

North Vietnamese quad 14.5-mm anti-aircraft guns

Parr and McManus assessed that there was only one approach safer than any other options and it was directly in the line of fire of six quad-14.5 mm anti-aircraft guns that were dug in and well-hidden on the hillside. Ralph lowered his nose and aligned himself on an approach for their third pass. There was anti-aircraft fire coming from one side of the ravine. It was wicked, unrelenting, and had evolved into a gauntlet for air force resupply aircraft. He quickly fixated on the second mortar position and scored a direct hit with a second canister of napalm. The weapon was delivered at nearly ground level; another direct hit.

After two more napalm passes, he now realized that he was left with only 20-mm external cannon fire as an offensive weapon. The mortar positions were obliterated and ultimately silenced by the napalm, however, more anti-aircraft guns were still 'alive' and positioned to cover the departure end leading up from the runway at Khe Sanh, which made the C-130s sitting ducks. Those transports were large targets for enemy gunners whose weapons were easily trained on the slow-moving targets.

The quads were furiously spitting fire as they tracked Ralph's aircraft attempting to lead him with their bullets, just like a sport shooter leads a clay target on the skeet range.

The NVA gunners scrambled to escape their previously hidden and 'safe' confines as Ralph went screaming by at better than 400 knots. With their muzzles flashing like lightning bolts, their guns unloaded a fierce stream of lead directly at his F-4 as he sped past, evading their firepower and preparing for the next target run. As Ralph turned to head toward the target, he saw something that caught his eye. He focused hard for a millisecond. There was a light-colored jagged rock protruding out of the hillside like a fist shooting out of the earth. He would use it as a pointer, or easily identifiable landmark for the remaining target runs.

He now maneuvered his way around for another setup. He was too low.[22] He looked up and right; there was a guy, an enemy, manning one of the six quad-barrel guns. The high speed of the F-4 made the gunner frantically rotate (relative to Ralph's aircraft) from his one to three o'clock position, then out of sight at his six, in less than three seconds.

The NVA had camouflage netting over their guns, supplanted in large holes, for protection from the formidable United States air attack. Ralph was low, too low. He saw the netting being tossed away from atop the guns. The gunner now feverishly cranked the hand wheel

[22] Ralph remembered, "I was too goddamned low but that was our only defense against the heavy anti-aircraft fire." Parr, Ralph S. personal interview. 30 November, 2011.

of his gun attempting to spin the long, hot muzzles around to get ahead of the F-4, attempting to track and lead his shots directly into the side of Ralph's aircraft.

The gunner struggled to crank his gun barrels around fast enough to lead Ralph's low and fast jet with his shots. The killer ammo poured from the four barrels with what seemed like thousands of rounds coming towards Ralph's cockpit and approaching close enough that he could see the non-tracer bullets as they passed by his canopy and over the cockpit. He was literally flying through a cloud of hot lead, with his aircraft as its intended destination.

Miraculously, he made it through the second pass. The Marine Corps battalion commander, who was monitoring the engagement between the FAC and Ralph, relayed an incredulous message to Ralph via the FAC. He said that he was canceling the mission due to safety considerations and overall survivability of Ralph's aircraft.

He said, "You've got to get out of there; they're shooting the shit out of you."

Ralph quickly responded, "You think I don't know that? I CAN SEE IT!"

Chapter 2
44 Years Earlier

There are a number of differing schools of thought regarding the recipe for traits found in a heroic fighter pilot like Ralph Parr, who begged for action and lived for daily improvement. The air force has always done an adequate job of administering personality and aptitude filters in its entry qualification examinations via the Air Force Officer Qualification Test (AFOQT), which is intended to pinpoint the precise Type-A people to best fill its annual flying requirement billets. Ralph would take it a step further—he'd say that it starts with an excellent upbringing by parents who teach 'The Golden Rule'[23] and instill good order and discipline in their children from day one. Most would accept that point.

Ralph was born in Portsmouth, Virginia, in a naval hospital on July 1, 1924, the son of Ralph S. and May Morrison Parr. He never had a cross word to say about either of his parents. They were great parents. Each

---

[23] (Bible Gateway) "Do for others what you would want them to do for you. This is the meaning of the Law of Moses and the teaching of the prophets." Matthew 7:12

played a significant role in his maturation by stressing the importance of integrity and sound moral judgment.[24]

His father was a U.S. Navy officer whose ship was in Norfolk at that time. They lived in base housing during most assignments, while his dad was at sea. His father would be home for three or four days at a time, long enough to replenish the ship's supplies, log some family time, and then head back out to sea.

His dad was a navy pontoon aircraft squadron commander in Manila in the Philippines. As a young boy, Ralph was amazed at how they'd tie the pontoon aircraft to buoys out in the harbor, allowing the aircraft to ride the waves while awaiting their next mission.

---

[24] Ralph remembered, "As an only child, I received total focus from my parents. Even though my dad was gone most of the time, he backed up Mom's disciplinary actions when he returned. I think it's so important to be involved in your children's daily lives. A part of that is slipping away today, leading to behavioral problems as kids mature."

A WWII pontoon aircraft landing.

His dad flew a single-engine aircraft fitted with pontoons for water landings. Ralph loved the sound of the prop beating the air into submission during the 'take-off roll' and eventual lift off from atop the white caps. There were plenty of pontoon aircraft stationed near island and coastal bases for him to see, as the aircraft-carrier concept was in its infancy at that time.

The Parr family's lifestyle was rather nomadic as they bounced from port to port during his father's naval career progression. His mom did not work outside the home, but she worked her tail off just the same around the house. Little Ralph tried to be 'the man of the house' when his dad was gone. Ralph started school in Mainland China but didn't recall much from those days, except that his dad was on a ship, anchored or docked on a river.

Ralph experienced the hardships of the Great Depression of 1929-39. Although he was only six years old, he knew that money was tight. They didn't do much as a family outside the house because they simply couldn't afford it. Near the end of the month, there was no money for food as his parents awaited their next paycheck on the 1st of the month.

He attended second grade in Manila, Philippines and went to third grade on the outskirts of London, England. His favorite time and place growing up was when he was about 10 years old in a local area suburb of London. He was finally old enough and allowed to get out on his own. He didn't often ride his bike around the neighborhood but just hung out with school friends, basically wandering around the neighborhood and peering through shop windows.

By the time he reached the fourth grade, his dad had finally received orders for a stateside assignment and they found themselves in Massachusetts. Then, they moved again, and he attended fifth and sixth grade in Maryland. Next, they headed back over the pond to attend seventh grade in London. His dad again received orders back to the states, and he returned to Maryland for eighth grade.

It was back and forth so many times that Ralph lost count. Ninth grade was back in England. Finally, they homesteaded for three years. He attended 10th through 12th grades in Maryland. After high-school graduation, he felt compelled to enlist in the army air corps to fulfill his burning desire to fly, and what he wanted to fly the most were fighters, in combat.

His first ride in an airplane was being strapped to his dad's lap, to celebrate his fifth birthday. It was an open cockpit and truly a life-changing event for him as it was then that he fell in love with flying. It was the wildest thing that he'd ever experienced. His dad let him handle the controls, even though he couldn't reach the rudder pedals. He let Ralph move the stick around, explaining and demonstrating how it controlled the movement of the aircraft. Ralph couldn't recall the aircraft designation, but he remembered that it was a seaplane in Manila, Philippines.

He knew that he wanted to be a fighter pilot when that 'flying seed' was planted on his fifth birthday.

On his sixth birthday, his dad said, "Son, how would you like to get another flight for your sixth birthday?" His father barely completed the 'day' in birthday when his mother's stern voice rang out from the next room, "Oh, no, you won't," she said sternly and with no apparent capacity to bend on her counter.

Apparently, she didn't want the only two living males in the family flying in the same aircraft ever again. She was totally cognizant of her husband's flying track record, thus effortless to put the kibosh on that idea. Ralph's dad had crashed but survived a couple of 'instances' in his early flying career. His dad never talked about them much and Ralph guessed that he couldn't blame him.

Before his love of flying took hold, Ralph stayed busy with normal chores associated with caring for the family dog. In fact, he wanted to play with the dog more than wanting to play baseball. It could be because the first time he tried playing baseball, the pitcher hit him in the elbow with a pitch. His elbow quickly swelled up and that single event skewed his love for baseball for the rest of his life.

Ralph played junior varsity basketball in high school. He enjoyed playing, but moving so often made it difficult to join a new team and adapt to the cohesive team spirit while still attempting to make new friends as an adolescent. He'd leave old friends behind and attempt to gain new ones with each move and then lose the new friends just as quickly when his dad received orders for a new assignment. It was truly the life of a dedicated military family, voluntarily packing up and moving so often, sometimes to undesirable locations.

Ralph played the violin at the insistence of his grandmother and against his better wishes. He simply was not good at it. First, he didn't care for it, which is very important if you want to improve on a task or action. Second, he was just trying to appease his grandmother. He had no choice; she made him practice all the time. So, he exercised his independence. He hated the violin so much that he thought he would learn to play the banjo. Well, no one liked the sound of the banjo as he practiced, so at that point they decided that enough was enough and let him be.

As a stay-at-home mom and having the time to experiment in the kitchen, his mother became an excellent cook. She was constantly baking for the family. An independent woman herself, his mom was proud of what they had, and she worked hard to keep things orderly and clean. She took on the role of the man and woman of the house with his dad being gone all the time.

His dad retired from the navy as a commander and went on to a second career as a captain on civilian freighters in the Atlantic. Then WWII broke out, and the navy pulled him back to active duty. He ran more than a hundred ship convoys to South America and Vladivostok, Russia. He was especially good at circumnavigating his way through the submarine barrier established near Russia. He was somewhat of a renegade as he wasn't one to go by the book.

He took this from his WWI and WWII shipping experiences and knowing that the Russians had copies of our books, depicting shipping strategies, plans, and tactics, he stressed the importance of remaining unpredictable to his mates. And unpredictable he was. He made his own procedural alterations, and, as a result, he spent more time than anyone leading convoys because he lost the least amount of ships.

He was one smart guy. He was number two in his Naval Academy class, able to solve complex math problems in his head. He once taught mathematics at the Naval Academy. He could go through five lines of code on a chalkboard and come up with the answer in his head. He found it difficult to understand why Ralph just didn't mop it up.

Ralph didn't realize how smart his dad really was until it was too late. His dad used encouragement to motivate Ralph, no matter what task he faced. During Ralph's flying training, his dad was at sea running convoys, so they didn't get to see each other often. Phone calls sure made Ralph's day though.

One day, he and his father had a heart-to-heart, father-son talk while his dad was home from one of his sea trips. He put his hand on Ralph's young shoulder and said, "Son, never pass up the opportunity to keep your mouth shut. That will keep you out of trouble." Ralph's ears perked up as he knew that this was a serious moment for them.

"If you're new in an outfit, never volunteer any information to the old heads unless you are specifically asked or they'll think that you're a know-it-all. After three months, through hard work and doing your job well, you will have established credibility with your peers and things will run a lot more smoothly," he said.[25]

Ralph knew that this wasn't a lecture. His dad knew that it was time for a life lesson and Ralph would live by those words for the rest of his life.

His dad died at the age of 57 when Ralph was in the midst of two Korean War tours in 1952. His mom died in 1958, at the age of 68. Each gone for the last 30 years of Ralph's life but the moral character and good judgment they'd instilled in Ralph was the foundation of their legacy that he openly carried to his grave.

Service to your country was an ingredient in their family blood. The only job Ralph's mother ever had was a service-oriented job. She drove an ambulance when she lived in France during WWI. She was always helping people, no matter what the circumstances. She was an amazing woman, generous to a fault. Ralph said that her kind heart and generosity was taken advantage of by acquaintances, but she didn't seem to care; it came with the territory.

Ralph's parents weren't the only guiding forces in his life. He was very close to his maternal grandmother. They had a lot of interaction growing up. His grandma was Scottish and actually lived in Scotland. She was well

---

[25] Ralph remembered, "My dad and I didn't experience too many heart-to-heart engagements, so when he explained the importance of keeping my mouth shut when I showed up at my new units until I had gained some credibility, I vowed to live by those words."

into her 90s when she passed. She took on the role of his mother when Ralph and his parents did most of their traveling and moving around the world. He stayed with her while his parents moved their household to a new destination.

She had six children: three boys and three girls, so she knew all about raising kids. Ralph learned early the reward for hard work. She helped instill that premise when Ralph stayed with her by paying him an allowance for doing chores around the house and keeping the yard up. He also had a paper route which forced him to interact with acquaintances he normally wouldn't know or talk to until he went to collect their newspaper payment. He was maturing in a hurry and realizing that he wanted to make a difference while earning a good living so that money wasn't always so tight. They were no different than any other military family—that's just the way it was. He knew that he had to do something good with his life and since the service was in his blood, the army air corps seemed like a perfect fit for him.

Chapter 3
Sunday Surprise

Everyone in Griffith Stadium that day knew his role. The wives walked into the Washington D.C. football venue together, chattering like a flock of birds. The 27,102 fans shoved through the turnstiles, ready to shout and clap, to watch and feel. The press box filled with reporters, prepared to scribble their notes. On the field, the players tried to keep warm. Some were stars, some weren't. It was the final pro-football game of the season for the Washington Redskins and the Philadelphia Eagles. It was cold. People stamped their feet. They could see their breath.

No one was thinking yet about Pearl Harbor. Kickoff was at 2 p.m.; 9 a.m. in Hawaii. Bombs had already fallen on the U.S. fleet, men had died, and war had come. In the stands, no one knew. The game was still everything. Philadelphia had taken a 7–0 lead on its first drive as announcements began to pour out of the PA system. Admiral Bland is asked to report to his office. Captain HX. Fenn is asked to report. The resident commissioner of the Philippines was urged to report. "We didn't know what the hell was going on," says Sammy Baugh, the Redskins' quarterback that day. "I had never heard that many announcements, one right after another. We felt something was up, but we just kept playing."

Only the boys in the press box had any idea. Just before kickoff, an Associated Press reporter named Pat O'Brien got a message ordering him to keep his story short. When O'Brien complained, another message flashed, "The Japanese have kicked off. War now!" But Redskins' president, George Marshall, wouldn't allow an announcement of Japan's attack during the game, explaining that it would distract the fans. That made Griffith Stadium one of the last outposts of an era that had already slipped away as those frigid fans would be the last to hear the devastating news.

The crowd oohed and cheered. When the game (and season) ended, a few hundred fans rushed the goalposts, with Washington winning 20–14. Baugh, with three touchdown passes, was the game's hero.

Then, everyone walked out of the stadium: the wives, the future Hall of Famer and the crowd. Outside, newsboys hawked the news. The world tilted, football lost all importance, and roles shifted. Women began fearing for their men. Reporters and fans would be soldiers soon. The world would not be divided into players and spectators again for a very long time. "Everybody could feel it," said Baugh.[26]

Ralph, now 16, sat in front of his radio at home in Washington, D.C., listening to the end of his beloved Washington Redskin's football game when the newsman broke into the broadcast with the horrific news. His dad leaped from his seat to lean closer to the radio so he

---

[26] (Price)

54

could hear precisely what the newscaster was saying.[27] The family was floored. Ralph couldn't believe what was happening. Did this mean flying fighters in combat might really be in his future? Only time would tell. For as long as he could remember, he wanted to fly. His fifth birthday present, flying an airplane while sitting on his dad's lap, remained the most memorable birthday of all. He contemplated his options.

The aviation cadet program appealed to him, but at the beginning of WWII, there was a requirement that cadets must have a college degree. Then on January 19, 1942, radical changes in the enlistment requirements and the training programs for all the armed forces were announced by A. James Casner, professor of Law, from information which he'd compiled as head of the emergency Student Defense Service Committee.

In general, the army and navy air corps had relaxed many of their old requirements in order to build up rapidly as large a body of men in the flying service as possible.

The navy and marine corps had encouraged enlistment by many new provisions. In particular, they had sought to stimulate applications from college men, by ruling that they may apply for officers' training before graduation and then delay active duty until they had received their degrees.

Finally, the army, coast guard, and Naval Supply Corps opened new drives to enlist increased numbers of

---

[27] Ralph remembered, "I'd never seen my father so visibly shaken in my life. I knew that everyone's life was about to change."

men for officers' training or for immediate service in the ranks.

Lowering the minimum age for enlistment to 18, the army air corps had, in addition, set aside the old requirement of two years of college training for all applicants. Instead, it ruled that candidates must, without exception, pass a revised aptitude test before admission into the air force.

A question typical of this aptitude test, which of course was only a sample and not to be found in the test, was recently released from Washington by the United Press: "If a hangar which is known to be 30-feet high casts a 20-foot shadow, what is the height of a signal tower which casts a 70-foot shadow at the same time of day?"

Furthermore, the army air corps announced that it will no longer be possible for men seeking admission to request service in any particular capacity, such as pilot or bombardier, but that they must expect to be assigned officially to the job for which they seem to be best suited.

Under the new rulings, the army air corps would accept the applications of married men and would induct them into the service under the same conditions affecting single men, provided they could show that their wives or others were not absolutely dependent upon them.[28]

Upon hearing the announcement, Ralph immediately went to the testing center to take the pre-qualification

---

[28] (Requirements for enlistment in U.S. Training Programs Relaxed)

entrance exams.[29] He passed the tests with flying colors, was accepted, and enlisted, being sworn in as a private. He was only 17 years old at the time, so his parents signed an age waiver, approving his entrance into the military.

Ralph always offered candid advice to aspiring Air Force Academy, Officer Training School, and ROTC cadets now sitting in the same boat that he was at that time in his life: "You have to be upfront and honest with yourself from the start. You need to find out what you're going to be good at. Whatever it is, you'd better like it because if you don't love what you're doing, you're never going to excel at it."[30]

Not yet qualified for pilot training, he started the cadet indoctrination process in Washington, D.C., and then headed to Miami Beach, Florida, for two months of intense basic training. After basic, he was sent to Wofford College in Spartanburg, South Carolina, to brush up on mathematics and aircraft identification for two months. He had no idea the roles that these schools would prove to play in his aviation future.

Then one day, he received what seemed like a message from heaven. The school's department head pulled him out of his daily studies to send him to the classification center, where he was administered even more testing. He passed the tests with high marks and qualified to attend pilot training.

---

[29] Ralph remembered with a grin on his face, "I guess I put enough round pegs in round holes and square pegs in square holes to pass the test."

[30] (Parr)

But administrative officials soon discovered that they'd lost his personnel records. With nowhere else to go, they moved him to Maxwell Field for the initial portion of pilot training. He entered that training wide-eyed and not really knowing what to expect. It wasn't long before he learned what hazing was. This was his first experience of having upperclassmen telling the 'newbies' what low-lives they were and how well they must treat their 'superior' upperclassmen. He quickly learned how to run the 'ratlines' (pronounced 'rattlin's') during the physical training, or PT portion of training while accepting an inordinate amount of hazing.[31]

Ironically, he lived about three blocks from the mess hall and didn't realize where it was located until he became a 'superior' upperclassman.[32]

From there, he journeyed to primary training in Lafayette, Louisiana, where he flew the Fairchild PT-23. It was powered by an enormous 220-horsepower radial engine and had two open cockpits with the instructor sitting up front and the student in the back. It utilized the old-fashioned Gosport tubes (a flexible one-way tube from instructor to student) for in-flight communication between the instructor and student. If the student annoyed the instructor enough, he would pull the mouthpiece from his mouth and hold it outside the cockpit in the

---

[31] Ratlines, pronounced "rattlin's", are lengths of thin line tied between the shrouds of a sailing ship to form a Ladder.

[32] Ralph remembered, "I found various ways to get my food from friends without ever having to go through the line at the chow hall until I was an upperclassman."

slipstream. The noise generated by the high airspeed nearly blew the student's eardrums out.

PT-23
The Fairchild PT-23 was used extensively as the Army Air Corps' initial pilot training aircraft.

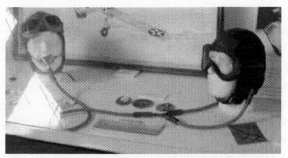

Gosport tube used for communication between instructors and student pilots in PT-23s.

There were about 125 cadets who entered primary flight school with Ralph, but only 53 graduated to the next phase of training. Ralph was now set for more basic training at Walnut Ridge, Arkansas, where he flew the BT-13, a training program notorious for a stunning 40-percent washout rate.

BT-13

While at Walnut Ridge, the leadership asked him if he would like to remain there and become an instructor. An instructor attempted to coerce him, "This is a first-class job to have."[33]

Ralph just couldn't see himself in a classroom any longer. He said, "No, I'd rather not. I want to go into combat." He was the first student in his class to solo in basic, proving his airmanship skills and generating the question about whether he wanted to become an instructor or not.

The next phase of training was advanced training, located in Blytheville, Arkansas, where he trained in AT-9s, another non-combat training assignment.

---

[33] Ralph remembered, "At every turn in the road, at the end of every phase of training, instructors would attempt to persuade me to stay at their base as an instructor. I couldn't seem to get it through their heads that I wanted to go to the fight and the sooner, the better."

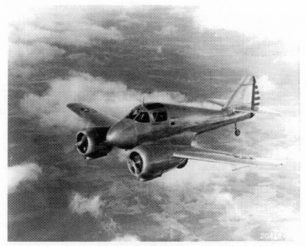

AT-9

The AT-9 advanced trainer was used to bridge the gap between single-engine trainers and twin-engine combat aircraft. The prototype first flew in 1941, and the production version entered service in 1942. The prototype had a fabric-covered steel tube fuselage and fabric-covered wings, but production AT-9s were of stressed metal skin construction. The AT-9 was not easy to fly or land, making it particularly suitable for teaching new pilots to cope with the demanding flight, characteristics of a new generation of high-performance, multi-engine aircraft such as the Martin B-26 and Lockheed P-38. Although the AT-9 originally bore the nickname 'Fledgling', it was more widely known as the 'Jeep'. Four hundred ninety-one AT-9s and 300 AT-9As were built before production ended in February 1943.[34]

---

[34] (Curtiss AT-9 Jeep/Fledgling)

Once again, he was the first student to solo and at the conclusion of the training, and was asked to become an instructor for the next class of students. Again, he said no; he wanted to go overseas to combat. Unfortunately, when everybody else's assignment was dispensed at assignment night, Ralph was the only one left seated without an assignment. He could see the writing on the wall. He was immediately made an instructor. In essence, he became a second lieutenant with silver wings on February 8, 1944 and was transitioned from being an aviation cadet in training one day to an instructor pilot with zero experience the next.

WWII was now in full swing. Newly assigned flight instructors were told to eliminate as few students as possible. Prior to 1939, the army air corps graduated roughly 1,200 pilots per year, but by 1942, the goal increased to 50,000 per year. At its peak, this rate would further increase to more than 74,000 annually. To help meet this high demand, a number of initiatives were taken.

By 1942, more than 50 civilian-contract flying schools were in operation. Along with expanding army air corps aviation training, entrance requirements were relaxed by lowering the minimum age to 18 and eliminating the college requirements.[35] The United States was preparing for the invasion of Europe in Britain. Considerable aircrew losses were anticipated, and they wanted to build up the aircrew force numbers as quickly as possible.

---

[35] (Ortensie)

Ralph accepted his new job as an instructor and took it very seriously. He normally trained five students from each class at a time. He attempted to fly with all five students each day but always managed to get at least four airborne, which was an incredible workload from an instructor's standpoint. If he could fly all of his students once during the day, then he could keep the same lesson plan, ensuring each student was exposed to standardized training on each sortie. It also made grading each individual even easier on the instructor.

Psychologically, Ralph could predict the student's mistakes by the time the third trainee was up to bat, and he knew the severity even before he started the maneuver. Ralph knew what to watch for after seeing problem that areas develop time after time. He learned to rotate the students' flying order on a daily basis in an attempt to avoid becoming overly rough on any one of them. It was a scheduling challenge but seemed to work rather well.

The best instructor pilots Ralph ever flew with always had pride in their work and were aggressive in nature. They had type-A personalities, and he carried the lessons, which he gleaned from them, with him every single day, on every single sortie, while molding his students to do the same.[36] Should you fail a check ride or an academic event, you must realize that there's no easy route. You have to be dedicated and have an extraordinary passion for what you do. It probably comes

---

[36] Ralph reflected, "In most cases, you unknowingly implement something that your previous instructors taught you on every sortie you fly."

back to this adage: if you don't like what you're doing, then change to a job that you like. If you find something you like, then improve daily.[37]

After instructing for a short time, Ralph knew that combat was where he belonged. He found himself getting thrown out of the group commander's office each time he begged to go to combat. Finally, one day, the group commander called him into his office and said that Ralph had finally gotten his wish to go to B-24 flight school. The commander held Ralph's orders in his hand.

He said, "Nobody else wants this assignment, so you've got it if you want it."

Ralph grinned and happily took the assignment and was soon off to Muroc AFB, California (renamed Edwards AFB in 1949) for B-24 flight training.

---

[37] (R. S. Parr, personal interview)

B-24

The B-24 was employed in operations in every combat theater during World War II. Because of its great range, it was particularly suited for such missions as the famous raid from North Africa against the oil industry at Ploesti, Rumania, on August 1, 1943. This feature also made the airplane suitable for long over-water missions in the Pacific Theater. More than 18,000 liberators were produced.[38]

Early in his new assignment, Ralph almost made a near fatal mistake and he wasn't even at the controls. He was a passenger on one of the initial training missions and airborne without wearing a parachute. While walking around the interior of the aircraft, he stepped on an open hatch. He fell and slid out of the open door and into the slipstream, up to his waist. His lower extremities were no longer in the plane; he was flailing, and his legs were slamming against the side of the fuselage. He locked his

---

[38] (Consolidated B-24D Liberator)

fingers on the gaping hatch opening, grasping the front side of the open hole. His white knuckles seemed welded to the inside of the freezing fuselage as he pulled himself into the safe confines of their craft. The whole ordeal was over in a matter of seconds, yet seemed like minutes to him. He sat motionless, in a trance, as his eyes stared down through the open hatch as the earth passed below. He prayed to God that he would never repeat that story.

At roll call the following morning, Ralph was called out of ranks and was told to see the commandant immediately. When Ralph reported in, the commandant said, "Who do you know at 4th Air Force Headquarters?"

Ralph said not only that he didn't know anyone in the headquarters, but he didn't even know where it was located. The commandant said, "It doesn't matter, you're getting shipped out of here. You're going to Ontario, California…tomorrow."

Stunned, Ralph said, "Where is that?"

The commandant said that he didn't know either, but Ralph could catch a bus the next day. So, away he went. Ralph climbed off a bus loaded with 2nd lieutenants reporting for P-38 pilot training, just outside Los Angeles that very next day.

The versatile P-38 Lightning performed many different missions during WWII, including dive bombing, level bombing, bombing through clouds, strafing, photo reconnaissance, and long-range escort. It first went into a large-scale service during the North-African campaign in November 1942, where the German pilots named it *Der Gabelschwanz Teufel* (The Forked-Tail Devil). When the Lightning began combat operations from England in September 1943, it was the only fighter with the range to escort bombers into Germany.

The Lightning truly shined in the Pacific theater; seven of the top eight scoring USAAF aces in the Pacific flew the P-38. On April 18, 1943, the long range of the P-38 enabled USAAF pilots to ambush and shoot down an aircraft carrying Admiral Isoroku Yamamoto, who was the planner of the Pearl Harbor raid and the commander of the Imperial Japanese Navy. The P-38 became the standard USAAF fighter in the Pacific theater until the closing months of WWII.[39]

The airfield at Ontario was covered with P-38s. Ralph had fallen in love with the P-38 when he was in high school. He'd seen them on the newsreels at the movies and thought that aircraft was the greatest thing since the invention of the wheel.

---

[39] (Lockheed P-38L Lightning)

P-38

After seeing the P-38s on the flight line, he said that there must be a mistake. Ralph wasn't sure that he really belonged there, but he wasn't going to tell anyone because he thought that maybe he could get a ride in one before they find him and send him to a different assignment. He checked into the bachelor's officer quarters as he readied for training. He had his first flight four days later and after he landed, it was confirmed that P-38 training was where he belonged. He'd never felt more relieved.

He was checked out in the P-38 at Ontario and received two or three times the normal amount of training since the war in Europe was winding down. He was flying the P-38L model featuring counter-rotating props that curbed the abnormal yaw produced in earlier models, where both props turned in the same direction and were equipped with compressibility flaps. It was one fine machine.

There were two things that he didn't really care for on the P-38. One was the aircraft brake system. The pilot had to push his foot flat to the floor just to begin braking. The other was the heating system. As you approached higher altitudes, the heating system was atrociously inadequate to combat the decrease in the outside air temperature. If you spent any time at high altitude, your feet grew so cold that they felt like they'd turned to blocks of ice.

Ralph would never forget the P-38 air-to-air gunnery briefing that he received one day. The training outfit employed towed targets for the gunnery training, which included in-depth prebriefings. After a briefing one day, Ralph nonchalantly hung around until everyone was out of the briefing room. He stopped the instructor as he attempted to walk by and asked, "Sir, what is a radius? Now, I'm not trying to be smart, but I really don't know what a radius is."

The instructor rolled his eyes and snapped, "Well, it's the difference between the reticle and the pipper!"[40] He might as well have ended his statement with, "You idiot!" because that's how Ralph felt.

Ralph said, "Okay." Still somewhat clueless, he stepped with his instructor to the aircraft to fly the training sortie.

---

[40] The reticle and pipper are two elements in an aircraft air-to-air gunsight.

Towed target used for air-to-air gunnery practice.

After the mission, the target was towed back to the base. It had eight holes in it and they were all Ralph's. No other student in his flight of four hit the target with their air-to-air guns. Ralph's instructor scratched his head during the debrief and said, "Why did you ask me about a radius?"

Ralph replied, "Because I really didn't know. I just did what you told me to do."

His gunnery accuracy, with now proven results, forced him to take a lot of ribbing from all the instructors and his peers from then on. No one else had even come close to hitting the target. The results of his success on that initial flight spread like wild fire. He knew he had a pretty good handle on things right out of the chute.

Chapter 4
Young Guns

Once finished with gunnery training, Ralph immediately headed to the east coast on board a C-47 transport bird for one night. He boarded a ship bound for Europe the next day, to fly missions in the European theatre. He climbed off the transport bird and checked into billeting to get some rest before the long boat ride across the pond the following day. Tensions ran high and adrenaline was flowing among all pilots that night. Nothing sounded better to the group than an ice-cold beer or a couple of cocktails to soothe their nerves and help them sleep.

The next morning, they were up early to board the ship. With literally one foot on the gangplank, one of the ship's crewmen stopped the line of pilots in their tracks. They waited for nearly 10 minutes, wondering what in the hell was going on before they were told that the war in Europe was coming to an end—it was 1945. Their orders had been reversed, and all were now being sent back to the west coast, headed to fly missions in the Pacific theatre.

They flew across the Pacific on a C-54, landing in Manila, Philippines, where they reported to a replacement depot at 0800 the next morning to the sounds of birds chirping, wild dogs barking in the distance and semi-muddy grounds from the nightly island showers that had rolled through the area earlier. A couple of days later, he was assigned to 7th squadron, 49th group at Lingayen Gulf. Ralph and his buddies were excited to be flying the P-38s. The jets were relocated there from another airfield in the south and they were awaiting the arrival of yet another sleuth of pilots from the states to fly them.

Now living in dark green tents with peaked roofs, there were four men to a tent, pitched in a 'mostly' secure area, however, he didn't feel totally secure. They were issued side arms, something Ralph wasn't accustomed to, and ordered to carry them at all times, even sleep with them.

On his first mission out of Lingayen Gulf, he flew as Bob DeHaven's wingman. Ralph knew that DeHaven carried an impeccable legacy. He had already witnessed this 7th Fighter Squadron transition to P-38s during July-September 1944 for the Philippine invasion. On 27 October, leading the 7th Squadron, DeHaven became one of the first AAF fighters to 'return' to the Philippines. Within seven days, he acquired four more victories. After leave in the United States, he rejoined the 49th at Lingayen as group operation's officer, serving into the occupation of Japan. By the end of hostilities, DeHaven would be credited with a total of 14 confirmed kills and one damaged.[41]

That day, young Ralph flew on Bob's wing up around some Japanese enclaves being 'cleaned out' in the jungles of Northern Luzon. Ralph was trying to be the

---

[41] (A WWII Screaming Demon of the 7th FS)

best wingman possible by not transmitting anything to DeHaven over the radios. Ralph could see sheets of concentrated 20-mm ground fire coming towards them, but then falling behind his aircraft, never finding their intended target. Finally, Bob's voice erupted on the inter-plane frequency saying, "Don't you see anybody shooting at us?"

Ralph said, "Yes, but they're not within 20 or 30 feet. If they get any closer, I'll tell you."

DeHaven didn't respond, however, he'd gotten quite a charge out of Ralph's reply and highlighted their in-flight dialogue during the post mission debrief. Everyone laughed. He had no idea that Ralph had so much situational awareness (SA). He figured that Ralph was just another clueless lieutenant on his wing, simply trying to fly his jet and stay in position. Situational awareness wasn't highlighted or even discussed back in those days, but there's a lot more emphasis placed on it today.

From a flying aspect, the P-38 performed extremely well, particularly below 15,000 feet. It had more than ample power, was fast, had rapid acceleration, and turned extremely tight. For Ralph, it was a joy to fly. Unfortunately, a P-38 pilot sits atop a big wing with two engine cells positioned directly alongside the pilot, restricting the pilot's visibility at 90 degrees looking down.

P-38 Lightning

The control response in the P-38 was fantastic. Comparing the P-51 Mustang, P-47 Thunderbolt and P-38 Lightning, overall the P-51 performance was probably the best platform for all the altitudes, visibility, engine response, etc., although it wouldn't turn quite as tight as the P-38 could.[42]

Japanese Mitsubishi A6M Zero

The Allies' nemesis in the Pacific air war, the Zero, is the most famous symbol of Japanese air power during

---

[42] (R. S. Parr, personal interview)

World War II.[43] The fighter first flew in April 1939, and Mitsubishi, Nakajima, Hitachi and the Japanese navy produced 10,815 Zeros from 1940-1945. It was produced in greater number than any other aircraft and its distinctive design and historical impact made the Zero an important machine in air power history.

The Japanese's advantage began to disappear as American tactics evolved. American pilots gained experience while fighting the Zero in China with the American Volunteer Group, known as the Flying Tigers, and at the Battle of Midway. The key to fighting the Zero was to stay out of dogfights, and instead use superior armament and hit-and-run diving attacks against the relatively fragile A6M. American fighters—introduced in 1943—were more powerful (2,000-hp engines), faster, and had much more firepower than the Zero. As allied pilots used their heavily-armed aircraft to advantage, the Zero's dominance ended. At the same time, the number of American aircrafts and pilots increased, and the number of experienced Japanese aircrew shrank. [44]

The distinct P-38 advantage that Ralph enjoyed most was the firepower it harnessed at his fingertips. The four .50-caliber guns and one 20-mm cannon mounted in its nose section could literally send a bar of hot steel streaming straight out the nose of the aircraft when you leaned on the trigger. If any portion of that stream found its target, something in or around the target aircraft was going to come unglued.

---

[43] Ralph remembered, "The Zero had such light wing loading that it could turn inside its own ass."

[44] (Mitsubishi A6M2 Zero Factsheet)

In 1945, Ralph's entire organization was transferred to Motobu Airfield on the island of Okinawa. That strategic move prepositioned the pilots and airframes closer to the bombing targets. They lived in tents there until a typhoon decimated the island. The locals called it the typhoon of the century and it nearly cost the United States a carrier in the gulf. Ralph realized the ferocity of the storm when a ridge pole came streaking like a missile, straight through the side of his tent, missing him by three feet.

When he crawled out of the sack to look outside, it was pitch black and palm trees were falling like bowling pins. He found it amazing how quickly the human mind and body transform into survival mode when faced with adversity. Shielding themselves from flying debris, some of the guys reluctantly, but quickly, sought shelter in nearby burial tombs. The tombs were laced with booby traps, so they had to be careful where they stepped. They couldn't tell if the traps were alive or dead. One thing for sure, the corpses were dead.

The tombs were stink holes, filled with corroding bodies. Upon their exit, the rest of the pilots wouldn't let them near for a couple of days because they carried the stench of death. During the typhoon, the caves shielded many of his buddies from the storm, but what a price to pay.

Safety was always a concern. Occasionally, the base would experience heavy artillery fire from nearby enemy emplacements, producing loud, bright bursts overhead, but thankfully, there were no enemy air attacks on the field during that time. That was about the time when

Ernie Pyle, a famous WWII journalist, was killed just two or three miles away.

Americans learned of Pyle's death at Ie Shima, just days after the death of President Roosevelt. On April 18, 1945, readers of the Washington Daily News opened their newspaper to find a large headline that read, '*Ernie Pyle Is Killed.*' There was a lengthy front-page article as well as articles that eulogized him and provided some personal anecdotes of his life. Over the next few days, Pyle's work continued to appear in its regular spot in the paper because he had recently submitted a new batch of articles, which the editors believed, merited the attention of his readers.

"*In addition to the story which appears here today, we will print several others which we have just received from Ernie on Okinawa. We believe that he would have wanted us to; as a great reporter, a great newspaperman, and a great person, he would have wanted his stories to go thru [sic], despite his tragic death.*"[45]

The day when the first atomic bomb was dropped, it stunned everyone. They had no idea that something of that magnitude was going to take place. In fact, when it did happen, everybody was talking and wondering about it. Lo and behold, the next one went off in Nagasaki. The capability America projected by dropping those two bombs proved that we possessed something that was never before imagined by mankind. By the time the second one detonated, everyone was pretty convinced that the war would wrap up right then and there.

---

[45] (Buljung)

United States President Harry Truman told British Prime Minister Winston Churchill that the United States planned to drop only one atomic bomb on Japan during their talks in Potsdam, Germany, in July 1945—one month before Japan suffered two attacks, according to a document at the Federal Archives Office in Berne, Switzerland.

Official documents confirmed that Truman ordered United States' strategic air forces to drop an atomic bomb on Japan on August 3rd or later. As for subsequent bombings, Truman told them to launch an attack 'as soon as the preparation is completed' but did not specify the number of bombs to be dropped.

The findings are expected to cast suspicion over why the second bomb was dropped on Nagasaki, which occurred three days after the first attack on Hiroshima on August 6, 1945.

The document was a memorandum, written by Max Petitpierre on February 1, 1947, then a Swiss state minister. Petitpierre took a leading role in Swiss diplomacy after World War II and later became the Swiss president.

The document covers talks held in Switzerland between Petitpierre and Churchill on September 18, 1946, after Churchill had retired.

According to the memo, Truman told Churchill that the United States was planning to drop the atomic bomb during the Potsdam Conference between the two leaders and Soviet leader, Joseph Stalin. Churchill later told Petitpierre that the U.S. was supposed to drop only one bomb on Japan and had not acted in accordance with plans.

During the Potsdam meeting, Churchill also observed from the sidelines as Truman informed Stalin of plans to use the atomic bomb. Stalin appeared not to understand the concept or how powerful the new invention (atomic bomb) was, Churchill reportedly told Petitpierre. Churchill also told Petitpierre that he thought Truman was not a very intelligent or skillful person.

Meanwhile, diaries of a member of the U.S. cabinet at that time confirm that Truman ordered the United States forces to stop using the atomic bomb after the second attack on Nagasaki, saying that it would be too horrible to kill another 100,000 people.

Japan unconditionally surrendered to the allied countries on August 15, 1945; six days after the bomb fell on Nagasaki.[46]

One of the eeriest missions Ralph ever flew was a sortie from Okinawa to Japan, a couple days after the bombs were dropped. It was tasked as a simple, low-threat reconnaissance mission on the north side, but this mission would leave images that burned in his brain. He would never forget the horror he saw and visions he unwillingly took to his grave. It was surreal to see Hiroshima and Nagasaki from the air, still smoldering as a result of the intensity of the atomic bombs. As he circled above in his P-38, he was nearly dazed as he stared at the ruins with thoughts of what it must have been like to be the recipient of such firepower.[47]

---

[46] (Truman told Churchill only one A-bomb was to be dropped)

[47] (R. S. Parr, personal interview) Ralph looked down at his lap, no eye contact, and spoke very slowly as he discussed

They flew a couple of 360s around each city and then headed back to Okinawa. This relatively 'vanilla' sortie turned dire in the next instant.

On his way back to Okinawa, things got crazy. Unbeknownst to him, there was a malfunctioning fuel line in one engine. Everyone else in the formation was pushing it up to make better time for home. As he scanned his cockpit instruments, Ralph quickly realized that his fuel state was below the planned fuel curve and was rapidly deteriorating. He thought that his fuel gauge must be malfunctioning but came to find out that the fuel gauge wasn't faulty at all.

Would he have to employ a lesson that he'd learned on an earlier flight with Charles Lindbergh, the master of fuel conservation?

Lindbergh had made history and worldwide headlines on 20 May 1927 at 7:52 am. He took off from Roosevelt Field, Long Island, New York in an aircraft, loaded with 450 gallons of fuel which were so heavy that he cleared the telephone wires at the end of the runway

---

what he saw on this mission. It was obvious that he was still greatly affected by those sights nearly 70 years later.

by only 20 feet. At 5:22 pm the next day, the Spirit of St. Louis touched down at the Le Bourget Aerodrome, Paris, France. Local time: 10:22 pm. Total flight time: 33 hours, 30 minutes, 29.8 seconds, with an average fuel burn of just over 13.4 gallons per hour. Charles Lindbergh had not slept in 55 hours.[48]

Ralph was lucky enough to fly on the same aircraft with Charles Lindbergh very early in his career. Ralph was a lieutenant at the time and both pilots were looking for a ride. They wound up sitting side-by-side, while they hitched a ride on a cargo plane from Andrews Air Force Base in Washington, D.C., to Roswell, New Mexico.

They were riding as passengers (not crewmembers), and during their course of conversation, the subject of cruise control and fuel management came up. Lindbergh was a master at getting the best performance out of his aircraft while burning the least amount of fuel. He'd just returned from a tour in the Far East, where he taught other pilots about fuel-conservation techniques during the cruise portion of flight. Ralph listened intently to what Lindbergh had to say because he held all the knowledge and experience on the concept at that time.

Ralph was totally stressing now, as anxiety set in and the thought of bailing out seemed inevitable. There was nothing but deep, blue ocean covered with white caps in all quadrants and no emergency airfields between his aircraft and Okinawa. He called his flight lead over the radio, informing him of his game plan. Ralph wanted to

---

[48] (Lindbergh's Transatlantic Flight: New York to Paris Timeline)

drop out of formation to run cruise control to conserve his precious fuel.

Ralph said, "Lead, this is three, I'm very low on fuel."

Lead replied, "You can't be low on fuel. We're all good here."

Ralph said, "It's either drop out of formation and pull the power back or not make it, and I'm not going down out here in the middle of nowhere!"

Ralph snatched Lindbergh's pet project from memory, hoping that he too could drastically reduce his aircraft's fuel-burn rate by employing Lindbergh's technique. It worked!

When land finally appeared as a small dot on the horizon, Ralph exhaled a huge sigh of relief. But his day was far from over. As he approached Okinawa, he called the tower declaring his fuel emergency. He requested a pattern clearance to shoot a circling approach to the south runway with a 180-degree turn to land back to the north.

The tower controller said, "Negative, you'll have to enter holding for sequencing. Standby for clearance." They were busy sequencing 52 inbound C-47s loaded with island supplies for landing. The line of inbound aircraft stretched like a train for miles.

As he peered through his canopy, he could see the small dots of airplanes off in the distance. Now perturbed, Ralph said, "Negative tower, I have to land now or I'm going to flameout and have to bailout."

The tower controller quickly replied, "You don't understand, these C-47s have priority."

Ralph replied, "Not in my emergency, they don't. I'm turning final now, clear me!"

Tower said, "I can't clear you. There's a C-47 right in front of you."

Ralph sternly replied, "You'd better tell him to take it around or I'm landing right on top of him. I don't have a choice. I don't have the fuel to make a go around."

At that instant, Ralph saw the C-47's twin engines generate a puff of smoke ahead of him as the transport pushed up his power to depart the pattern, allowing Ralph to land in his place.

The C-47 pilot chimed in on the radio and said, "Roger, pee shooter, we're getting out of your way now."

Ralph genuinely thanked him.

When Ralph shut down the engines, the crew chief measured the gas in his tanks and said that he had less than five gallons remaining. That's a mere few minutes' worth of fuel. You never know if it's a gauge problem or not when the tanks run that low. He was extremely lucky as Charles Lindbergh's fuel saving lesson had saved his life and airplane that particular day.

Soon, news that the war was coming to an end spread like wildfire. He'd survived his first war as a new lieutenant but more importantly, learned to adapt to adverse situations while making well thought-out decisions, ensuring his longevity.

Interestingly, in WWII, there was only one unit from all our services that didn't get their socks shot off during the first air battles. That small unit was run by one of Ralph's heroes, a man named Claire Lee Chennault, who led the famed 'Flying Tigers' and the United States 14th Air Force against the Japanese in China and Burma during World War II. He was a charismatic airpower theorist and a controversial leader, who at times disagreed with official doctrine and his superiors.

Chennault learned to fly in the army after World War I and became the army air corps' chief of pursuit training in the 1930s. He believed strongly in the value of fighter aircraft, and his theory of 'defensive pursuit' argued that fighters could destroy attacking bombers. Chennault openly disagreed with his superiors, who believed that bombers would be unstoppable in future wars. By 1937, poor health and disputes with top commanders led Chennault to retire from the army.

Quickly, though, he joined a small group of American civilians training Chinese airmen in their battle against Japan. Chennault later helped persuade President Franklin Roosevelt to send American aircraft and volunteer pilots to assist China a few months before the United States was at war.

Chennault's '1st American Volunteer Group' (AVG)—better known as the Flying Tigers—began training in the summer of 1941, and they fought the Japanese for six months after Pearl Harbor. As the United States' Army Air Forces absorbed the AVG in 1942, Chennault rejoined the army. He became a major general and commanded the AVG's successor, the 14th Air Force, until almost the end of the war. In this influential post, he dealt personally with Chinese Head of State Chiang Kai-shek and President Roosevelt.[49]

Ralph felt that the Flying Tigers were the most prepared who were going into WWII. They were the only ones who didn't lose their hat, ass, and spats when they

---

[49] (Maj. Gen. Claire Chennault)

first got into combat. Chennault trained his pilots by telling them what they needed to know, then demonstrated how to execute what he'd taught them. That's why our fighter pilots are far better trained today. Ralph tried to emulate Chennault throughout his career.

At the end of WWII, Ralph's outfit was moved north to Japan. It moved to Hokkaido Air Base, where he continued flying P-38s for a short time. During the move, a lot of paperwork was lost from all the squadrons. That misstep would have a deep impact on Ralph, as the paperwork stating his desire to stay on active duty was part of the lost pile. When the time came for him to sign up to stay in the air force, Ralph wasn't notified because no one knew it. The date came and went; hence his orders were already cut, leading to his impending separation.

His commander called a dejected Ralph into his office and said, "We can fight it."

Ralph shrugged and said, "I guess it was meant to be. I'll just go along with it."

He separated from active duty and immediately went over to sign up in the Reserves at Andrews AFB with two friends, Bill Hall and Robert P. Pasqualicchio. The Reserve unit only had a couple of P-51s and the guard said that they should come to their unit to fly P-47s,

P-51

which appealed to the three young guns because the guard had more aircraft; meaning all three could fly more often.

P-47

Ralph had made a clean transition from active duty to the guard. All seemed to be going well until one day, a navy guy came 'hot dogging' at Ralph and his flight flying their 'Jugs' (P-47s). The Navy F-8F pilot was playing yo-yo with Ralph's flight, visibly laughing as he danced his aircraft all over the sky, in and around Ralph's four-ship formation. The navy pilot rocked his wings, indicating his desire for Ralph to join on his wing.

Ralph pulled his aircraft up and rolled over the top of him and parked his aircraft in perfect position on his right wing. The shocked navy pilot stared from his cockpit, his eyes were big as tea cups and mouth hung wide open after seeing Ralph's maneuver. Ralph's wingman, Bill Hall, thought that he could do the same thing, except his maneuver was a little too tight and his wing overlapped with the navy pilot's wing, taking the guy's wing's tip off as he attempted to move into position.

Hall knifed about two feet off the left wing of the Navy F-8F. The chunk of the wing with its one jagged edge was sent violently spinning, like an out-of-control Frisbee headed for the ground. They all about shit themselves.[50]

After the flight landed, Ralph visually picked up a staff car cruising out on the ramp (aircraft parking area). As the flight taxied by, the staff car spun around like it hit a patch of ice and followed them back to parking. Ralph really couldn't see who was at the wheel, but he knew that whoever it was, they were pissed. He realized that nothing good was in his future.

When they reached their parking spot and were in the chalks, engines shut down; an irate group commander approached them. After only a few minutes (which seemed like an eternity to Ralph), the commander left the

---

[50] Ralph sat back in his recliner, openly laughing about the midair nearly 70 years later, but he thought that the ensuing punishment would end their flying careers that day.

somber pilots with their heads hanging low as he elaborated on what his senior leaders were discussing regarding the impending punishment that would affect their future aviation careers. He said that court martial and flight evaluation boards (stripping them of their wings) were the two main topics.

Ralph asked, "What happened to the navy guy? He started it all!"

So, they checked. A navy liaison told them that the F-8F pilot landed safely at their base and wrote the airplane up[51] as having 'a broken wing tip' and left the aircraft in its parking spot. He got nothing as far as punishment. It wasn't funny at the time but would be years later.

After flying with the guard for four or five months, Ralph discovered that going to school in the daytime, then flying nights and weekends was not conducive to making top grades. Although he wasn't failing any classes at the time, he realized that mediocre grades were not going to get him very far in the long run.

Ralph knew that he couldn't stop flying, so he needed to decide right then and there what he really wanted to do with his life. He figured that he'd better get back on active duty and stick with flying, since it had been his life-long dream.

He soon applied to return to active duty through the Pentagon and received a call almost immediately.

---

[51] Notations the pilot adds to the aircraft's maintenance forms after landing, describing an aircraft malfunction requiring the attention of maintenance personnel.

The Pentagon rep said, "Hey, I understand that you're interested in coming back on active duty. Well, we are short on pilots." So, he reentered the fledgling (one-year old) air force in January of 1948 and proceeded with his career.

Ralph's transition to the jet age was a very exciting time in his life. He went to the 33rd Fighter Group at Roswell, New Mexico. They were currently flying P-51s, but he knew that they were slated to transition to early model F-84Cs. They were programmed to receive them next.

The F-84, the USAF's first post-war fighter, made its initial flight on February 26, 1946. It began rolling off the production lines in June 1947, and by the time the production ceased in 1953, approximately 4,450 'straight-wing' F-84s (in contrast to the swept-wing F-84F) had been built. In addition to being used by the USAF, many were supplied to allied nations, participating in the Mutual Security Program. During its service life, the F-84 became the first USAF jet fighter that was able to carry a tactical atomic weapon.

F-84C

The airplane gained its greatest renown during the Korean War, where it was used primarily for low-level interdiction missions. Almost daily, the F-84 attacked enemy railroads, bridges, supply depots, and troop concentrations with bombs, rockets, and napalm.

After flying P-51s for about five months, the new, bright, and shiny F-84s rolled in and were assigned to his squadron. The ops officer walked out of his office one day and said, "Okay, you four guys come here," as he pointed at Ralph for inclusion in that group. He handed each of them a 'dash one' (the aircraft flight manual) and said, "Take the 'dash one' out there and study the exterior of the aircraft during the walk-around. Then sit in the cockpit and practice the checklists until you think that you can hack it, but be damn sure that you give (the 'dash one') back to the crew chief before you launch because we only have four of them."

That was a loose way of getting checked out in a brand-new aircraft, but a formal ground-training program was not yet developed. The ground training unit wouldn't arrive there for at least another month, but they wanted to start flying the airplane. Ralph and his three buddies did the best with what they had and felt obliged to do so.

Chapter 5
Tank Busting

The Korean War began on 25 June 1950 and lasted until 1953. The North Korean People's Army, equipped with Soviet weapons, crossed the 38th Parallel to take over South Korea. The United States' military presence in the Far East was undermanned, and its equipment was outdated except for the air force, which had a mixture of World-War-II piston-powered aircraft and a reasonable number of Lockheed F-80 jet fighters. The North Koreans and their Soviet advisers were under the impression that President Harry Truman and the United States did not consider South Korea to be within the United States' sphere of influence.

The United States used airpower to slow down and then stop the invaders. On the 26th and 27th of June, the top priority was to evacuate U.S. citizens and top ranking South Korean officials out of Seoul. A Norwegian freighter happened to be in the Inchon Harbor, getting most of the people out on the first day. The remaining personnel were flown out by C-54 transports on 27 June. On that day, the North Korean air force made an aggressive move to interrupt the air traffic in and out of Kimpo Air Base (Seoul).[52]

As the news broke, Ralph was ferrying an airplane from one base to another. He arrived back at Otis AFB, Massachusetts, and walked in at eight o'clock in the morning to find that a pilot meeting was scheduled for ten o'clock. His squadron commander, Major Glenn T. Eagleston, a leading WWII Ace, would lead the meeting.

He said, "Looks like we're in a war." As the meeting ended, they all stood. As Major Eagleston walked by Ralph, he patted him on the back and said, "Ralphie, you go sic 'em. This is just up your alley." He picked his quota of pilots and said, "By eleven o'clock tomorrow morning, 16 of our pilots will be headed to the Far East."

The next morning, a civilian charter airplane came to pick the 16 pilots and off they went. They sped over the Pacific headed for Japan with short refueling stops along the way.

Once the pilots arrived in Japan, the Air Force soon realized that the only air cover available was from several flights of F-80s and a flight of North-American F-82 Twin Mustangs, one of which scored the first victory of the Korean air war. U.S. jet aircraft lacked the necessary range for combat over Korea. After a flight from Japan, they had only a few minutes over the target area. As a stopgap, the tiptanks were increased in size to give the F-80s additional flying time.[53]

Unknown to Ralph, this would be his first of two tours in Korea. This initial tour would have him flying F-

---

[52] (Thompson)

[53] (Thompson)

80s with the 49th Fighter Wing, the same unit he'd flown P-38s with during WWII. He had only five hours of combat time when he passed his tenth hour in the aircraft, and that was after ferrying it on two long hops.

F-80

He was a 'newbie' in the jet. The F-80 didn't carry a very heavy bomb load, but it was jet-powered and could get out there much faster than the prop-driven airplanes of days gone by. It also happened to be the only jet on the scene at that time. It was the best aircraft they had available.

The momentum of the North Korean forces allowed them to compress the United Nations' forces into a narrow perimeter around Pusan. The Battle of Pusan Perimeter was a large-scale battle between United Nations (UN) and North Korean (NK) forces, lasting from 4 August to 18 September 1950. It was one of the first major engagements of the Korean War. An army of

140,000 UN troops, having been pushed to the brink of defeat, were rallied to make a final stand against the invading North Korean army, 98,000 men strong.[54]

The perimeter defenders were sustained by aircraft of the Far East Air Force, which provided close air support and interdiction of supplies. On 15 September, General Douglas MacArthur used the newly arrived 1st Marine Division to make a daring amphibious landing at Inchon. This caught the North Korean military completely off-guard and created a lightning-fast thrust to the east by the marines to cut off enemy supply lines. The result was a mass retreat by the North Koreans and breakout from the Pusan Perimeter.[55]

Back in the squadron, Ralph and the others were meandering their way through many hurdles during the opening months of the war. One of the issues was the lack of personal equipment at that time. Scarcity is the first word that comes to mind, but that's an incredible understatement. The only reason Ralph had a pair of flight gloves was because he just happened to bring a pair of his own when he deployed. Some of the guys in his flight were literally flying with football helmets which they'd purchased at the PX (Post Exchange). To create 'falsies,' they scooped portions of the sponge/rubber head protection out to make room for their heads.

As part of the 49th Fighter Wing, he was assigned to the 7th Squadron. The squadron leadership looked at his stellar 'Form 5' (record of flight evaluations) and said

---

[54] (Battle of Pusan Perimeter)

[55] (Thompson)

that they were going to make him a flight commander because he had a lot of jet time.

The instructor cadre asked, "How much F-80 time do you have?"

Ralph replied, "I don't have any."

They said, "Oh. Well, how much T-33 time do you have?"

Again, he replied, "I've never flown that one either."

They said, "We'll set you up in a training program requiring five transition rides, then give you four air-to-ground gunnery rides followed by two formation rides. Then we'll clear you to go to Southern Japan and let you start flying combat missions."

Being the new man in the outfit, Ralph adhered to his father's earlier advice: "Keep your mouth shut and your eyes and ears open for at least the first two or three months. If you don't, they'll think that you're a loud-mouth know-it-all...and don't ever volunteer any information unless you are asked." Ralph employed his advice.

On his first transition ride, they had one of the young lieutenant 'hot rods' waiting for him to take off. He would 'try Ralph on for size' to see how he would respond in all flight regimes. Ultimately, he was there to see if Ralph could handle the airplane. He never saw the actual result of his evaluation, but when Ralph landed, the squadron leadership said that they were waiving all remaining transition rides.

The next morning was his first of four air-to-ground gunnery rides. When the scores came back from the first sortie, his target showed more than 80 percent hits. Their top gunnery instructor's target had 35-40 percent hits, so they immediately jumped on Ralph's case for not shooting at the right target. He kept his mouth shut. When the range officer finally got back that afternoon around five o'clock, the guys were all over him for allowing Ralph to attack the wrong target.

He said, "I didn't allow him to attack the wrong target. That's the target he was assigned."

One of the troops that he had deployed with was standing nearby with another buddy and said, "Well, that sounds about right. I don't know if you knew it or not, but Ralph was in the worldwide gunnery meet last month, and the team placed second!"

Ralph was told the next morning that he could ferry an airplane down south. This was his introduction to combat missions in Korea.

He was assigned to K-2 airfield. It was just outside Taegu. When he arrived, they had 4,500 feet of pierced steel planking, referred to as PSP, for a landing strip. It had sand and mud under it, making for sporty landings. It hollowed out in spots and occasionally got so rough that they would inadvertently snap a nose wheel off during takeoff.

The pilot force wanted to extend the runway for safety reasons, but there was a town adjacent to the airfield and the villagers objected to giving up a portion of their village to enlarge the airfield. Unfortunately, one airplane didn't make the landing one time, and it crash landed in the village and a portion of the village was decimated. The villagers quickly decided that maybe they should sell a portion of the town, enabling the Americans to build an additional 1,500 feet of the runway, which immensely aided air operations.

At the time, living conditions were not optimum as he was once again living in a tent. The runway ran parallel to the valley at the very bottom of a 2,500-foot-hill and the squadron members pitched huge tents on the side of the hill. The noise normally heard in a combat zone made sleeping nearly impossible. The thing that bothered them most was the constant enemy fire that they were taking from atop the hill. The enemy fire was putting holes in their airplanes while in the traffic pattern around the airfield. That really pissed them off.

The air force convinced the army that if the aircraft continued receiving damage while arriving and departing the airfield, they wouldn't be able to support the army troops with close air-support missions, even if they were only five miles down the road and fighting like mad. The army was urged to consider overtaking the top of the hill to ease the constant enemy fire raining down on the airfield. The army listened. They took over the hill and the enemy fire became non-existent from that point forward.

The F-80 was a remarkable aircraft for its time. It carried a full armament of weapons, including .50-caliber machine guns, napalm, 250- and 500-lb. bombs, as well as five-inch, high-velocity, air-to-ground rockets, also referred to as 'Hi-Vars'. A normal bomb load would be two or four Hi-Vars. The critical factor was aircraft takeoff weight. They basically carried the maximum payload allowed to safely get off the ground, with temperature and pressure altitude used as entering arguments for takeoff performance charts. The higher the temperature and/or pressure altitude, the less weight or payload they could carry.

The North Korean Air Force was decimated in the first few days of the war. The MiGs hadn't even shown up yet. Three weeks after the Inchon landing, the United States' Eighth Air Force began withdrawing to the south. The Soviet-built swept wing MiG-15 appeared in significant numbers during November, and for the first time, communist forces threatened to gain air superiority.[56]

Ralph flew missions up north three times and found MiGs each time. The F-80s were loaded primarily with air-to-ground weapons and were no match for the air-to-air capabilities of the MiGs. Ralph would simply play with them and then fly away in an attempt to harass the opposing pilots. They stopped these types of missions since they didn't bode well for the longevity of him or his aircraft.

Flying air-to-ground missions in the F-80 could get a little exciting at times. Ralph was nearly killed on three separate occasions—in one week—during this tour. The small-glass canopy of the F-80 only allowed for a slight portion of your head to be seen by enemy gunners or fighters. In one week, Ralph saw the bullet coming at him three separate times. Luckily, the first one glanced off the armor plate in front of him. None of those bullets were tracers. He saw the puff of smoke and the center flame blast from the muzzle of the gun, followed by the bullet coming straight at him. It slammed into the armor plate in his windscreen, narrowly missing his head.

The second time, Ralph watched an enemy on the ground un-sling his rifle from his shoulder as he walked

---

[56] (Thompson)

down the road. As Ralph approached at low altitude, infantryman frantically pulled up, taking aim at Ralph's F-80. At such low altitude, Ralph saw him cock the bolt on his rifle and fire. Again, Ralph saw the smoke burst from the enemy rifle, then fire leaping toward his jet from the end of the gun. The solid streaking projectile smacked the Plexiglas canopy with the loudest noise that he'd ever heard from within the cockpit and ricocheted off. It scared the shit out of him. Ralph took his gloved hand and rubbed the damaged canopy. The charred, jagged glass sliced through his glove like a razor.

On the third day, Ralph saw the bullets coming at him again. This was becoming a trend. He was in a steep turn when the bullets began appearing from the right side of his aircraft. He was once again at extremely low altitude. At that point, he leaned his head down in the cockpit to reach the homing device near the floor and between his rudder pedals. *Inside the cockpit, I heard a loud boom, exactly like the one I'd heard on the sortie two days earlier,* Ralph thought to himself as his head was nearly between his knees. *I think that one was a direct hit.*

As he straightened back up in the cockpit, he saw a large bullet hole in the side of the canopy, at ear level. He quickly scanned his instruments and snapped his head to look to the other side of the canopy, and there was another bullet hole in the exact opposite side of the canopy. A single bullet had made it completely through his canopy precisely where his head had been just a second before. It was his lucky day.

Ralph had survived after taking three hits: one each on a Monday, Wednesday, and Friday of the same week.

After cheating death three times in a row, he went straight into ops (the flying operations building) and requested a three-day 'R and R' pass for some rest and relaxation. At the time, Ralph thought that someone was trying to tell him something and he'd better listen.

The F-80 was an excellent air-to-ground platform. Even though he preferred the air-to-air fight, Ralph quickly mastered the skills required for air-to-ground success. One day, he was out, looking for targets of opportunity. The weather was great with good visibility. He found that if he could peel the top off a tank by hitting it right at the base of the turret with concentrated .50-caliber rounds, the top would literally come off and the tank's sides would blow out. He ended up taking out three tanks using his new technique in a single day. He rushed back to tell his squadron mates about his newfound success, and some of them employed the same technique with similar results.

That month, he destroyed 87 enemy trucks. The trucks would come lumbering down the highway in the dark, filled with supplies. They would have an armored vehicle waiting for them to transport the ammo. Once the American pilots figured out the enemy routing, those trucks and armored vehicles were sitting ducks for the ensuing onslaught of airpower. In an attempt to trump U.S. tactics and save some of their armor, the North Koreans camouflaged their tanks by blowing a hole in the front of a house. Then they'd slip right underneath the thatched roof for protection from air attack by backing their tank into seclusion.

Now, it was Ralph's play. How do you find tanks that are hidden inside houses? He flew his jet down to nearly the same level as the tanks in order to visually spot them in their 'hidden' parking spots. He had to fly low enough, so he could look into the front of the house and under its roof as he flew by. Once spotted, he kept his eye focused on that particular house while getting set up for a strafing run. He pulled his F-80 hard around in a climbing turn, and then he lowered the nose to line up on the house his eyes had never left. He unleashed a burst of .50-caliber rounds into the thatched roof and the house would turn to ashes as it burst into flames, destroying the tank and killing everyone inside, while ultimately leveling the house and anything nearby. The secondary explosions from the tank's ammunition did nearly as much damage as his initial strafing hits.

It wasn't common knowledge at the time, but the North Koreans had pushed far south and lost about 80% of their armor. Some politicians back in the states referred to American efforts as 'police action'. However, Ralph thought that whenever you start deliberately killing people on both sides, those actions nix the police action—it's now all about war. This was a real fight, not a game.

Unfortunately, by using the term 'police action', they put restraints on American forces as far as what they could and couldn't target and where they could go, including new rules of engagement once the pilots and planes were in place. Ralph felt that this wasn't in our best interests from a flight safety standpoint.

Chapter 6
Can I Run Any Faster?

Everyone took a turn as the fighter guy, playing the role of Forward Air Controller, or FAC. When Ralph's turn came around, they provided him with a radio and a Jeep, designed for calling in airstrikes in support of ground forces.

U.S. Army Jeep used by Forward Air Controllers during the Korean War.

The intensity and frequency of using ground FACs increased when the Chinese entered the war in 1950. The Chinese had 180,000 troops in the fight and sent their troop mass rambling right down the center of Korea. They called it the Chosen Retreat. Our marines were taking a shellacking.

Ralph was in his Jeep one day, parked at the base of a mountain about three miles from the front lines, trying to catch a glimpse of the enemy's progress. The extreme number of Chinese and massive firepower that they employed enabled them to run through the marines and right by his position in no time at all. They had two radio jeeps with one FAC and one South-Korean interpreter each. They were based out of Kunueri. They had traveled about four or five miles, slowly approaching the front lines.

Near 02:00 in the morning, the crisp air enhanced the broadcast of all available noises, including their Jeep. They could hear the crickets and birds chirping as they traveled at a snail's pace, moving as quietly as they could, with their Jeep in low gear. Suddenly, all of the sounds stopped. The silence made the hair on the back of Ralph's neck stand up. He knew that the only thing that could make those noises stop was some sort of movement. He wasn't sure if it was his Jeep creeping along or if something else had silenced the jungle that night.

Suddenly, a Chinese infantryman jumped out from behind a tree with a burp gun. He took one step forward and bumped into the right front headlight of Ralph's Jeep.

Chinese Burp Gun

His headlights were off, but they were running with two little night lights mounted under the front bumper that were shining straight ahead. They were mounted very low to the ground for concealment. They normally drove through the terrain with the lamps rather than use the bright headlights of the Jeep for concealment purposes.

Ralph had to stop the Jeep suddenly to keep from running over the infantryman. Each being surprised by the other, the infantryman was wielding his burp gun toward the Jeep. Ralph was overly cautious. The Chinaman motioned his machine gun at them, not speaking but persuading Ralph and his interpreter to get out of the Jeep. Ralph nodded his head and slowly waved his hand as though he would comply with the aggressor's demands.

At the same time, Ralph slowly reached down and grabbed the stick shift, placing the Jeep's transmission in reverse while simultaneously stomping down on the accelerator and dumping the clutch. The Jeep lunged backwards at a high rate of speed as the adrenaline pumped through all three of the men's veins.

The Chinaman immediately swung his gun in the Jeep's direction while pulling the trigger. The muzzle fire lit up the entire area and the noise was astounding as he shattered the entire windshield with multiple rounds in a single burst of gunfire. The bullets went through the windshield and right between Ralph and his interpreter riding in the passenger seat. The Jeep was a very narrow vehicle and it was amazing that neither of them was hit by the hot lead. They were covered in shards of glass from the broken windshield while Ralph was actually spitting glass lodged between his clenched lips.

As the Chinaman pulled the trigger and fire leaped from the muzzle, the burp gun recoiled, forcing him to stumble backward over the roots of the tree that he'd popped from behind seconds earlier. The force of the recoil and exposed tree roots made him tumble to the ground like an unconscious boxer. Ralph quickly completed his bootlegger turn, and they sped away into the safety of darkness and out of sight.

They continued driving south as fast as they could. They knew that they'd just about met their maker less than a minute earlier. With their hearts still racing, accompanied with labored breathing, it was a welcomed sight to see their squadron mates milling about as they approached the camp. When the guys in the yard saw the Jeep all shot to hell, they were full of questions and wondered what in the hell had happened.

The next morning, about three-quarters of a mile down the road from where the incident had taken place the night before, Ralph decided to drive over a nearby hill for a better viewpoint of the valley below. It was extremely steep and he had to search for the right trail, otherwise the chances of rolling the Jeep increased exponentially. Ralph had surveyed the road earlier from the air and remembered what it looked like. He slowly climbed the hill and saw their 'sister' Jeep with its FAC and interpreter on the far side of the dry-lake bed. Ralph stood up looking around and thought that maybe he could slide down the hill, attempting to get as close to the other Jeep as he could so he could talk to them.

Suddenly, there was a WHOOSH and BANG! He felt the air compression, that normally accompanies a speeding bullet, zing by his head followed by the delayed, deafening sound of a high-powered rifle. He immediately dove for cover. His interpreter was with him and they both hit the ground in a low crawl. They scurried along in several directions to evade any subsequent gun fire.

The enemy was shooting at the guys in the other, trying to stop them. Ralph and his interpreter watched as their counterparts drove their Jeep abeam his current position before they were forced to stop. They were forced out of the Jeep by the Chinese men at gun point. Then they were forced to their knees on the road, behind the Jeep. One enemy fighter lifted the flap on his holster, pulled out his pistol, and placed it against the back of the FAC's head. He pulled the trigger instantly, killing the FAC, and then the assassin methodically killed his interpreter in the same execution style.

The bullet that had Ralph's name on it had missed his head by less than two inches.

Ralph looked at his interpreter and said, "We gotta get the hell out of here!"

They raced back through the enemy lines as fast as they could, remaining as covert as possible. They were on the run for nearly two days. The name of the game at this point was survival. Near-death experiences affect individuals in many different ways. For Ralph, it was sobering. They had to stay secluded and not get caught.

Ralph was the last American to safely make it out of Kunueri. They escaped after dark a few nights later. In fact, there was a cop standing on top of a half barrel, directing traffic at the last intersection as the traffic congestion resembled a hurricane evacuation back in the states.

When they finally arrived at their new camp, one of Ralph's feet felt funny. He had a deep gash down his lower leg that had bled down and along his leg and inside his boot. His sock was warm and squishy. The army colonel at the camp told him to go to the medic and get his foot cleaned up so the doctor could look at it. Some guys were just sitting around, chatting, when Ralph overheard that there was a C-47 that had landed earlier and just unloaded ammo and supplies. It was still on the field. The medics were now loading patients on it for evacuation. Ralph asked them if he could catch a ride south to reconnect with his unit.

They said, "Sure, hop on." So he did.

Ralph's injury wasn't caused by the bullet that had sped past him. A chunk of jagged rock had ricocheted off the ground and punctured his leg, slashing it wide open. He dumped his ruined boots in the trash. He jokingly asked the medic if his leg injury warranted a purple heart.

He said, "Nope, not this time, Charlie!"

Ralph said, "That's alright, I don't have time for that right now anyway."

Being a ground FAC was very different from flying and fighting. It was a God-awful time up in the front lines and Ralph found himself asking what the hell was a fighter pilot doing on the ground?

Somebody later asked Ralph, "Were you scared?"

He replied, "Hell, yes, I was scared. But when you're scared, the only thing you ask yourself is, 'Can I run any faster?' And then, you run faster!"[57]

During his first tour, Ralph ended up flying 165 air-to-ground missions in the F-80 before he was selected to go back to George AFB, California, in June 1951. He was elated about going to train in the new F-86 Sabre.

---

[57] (R. S. Parr, personal interview)

Chapter 7
F-86s in Korea

Ralph arrived at George AFB[58] in sunny southern California, eager to fly the F-86 with another pilot who'd served in his same squadron during Ralph's first Korean War tour. Maj. Frederick C. 'Boots' Blesse and Ralph were unmatched in their desire for self-improvement. They decided to perform some inflight tests to see if two pilots flying relatively similarly performing aircraft—in their case, F-86 versus F-86—could simulate MiG-15 versus F-86 dogfights, hoping to develop tactics providing one an edge over the other.

Aircraft armament also played a key role in their F-86 tactics development that was dependent on aircraft performance and weapons' capabilities. The F-86 carried six M-3 .50-caliber machine-guns. The M-3 was a later version of the M-2 used in World War II. The MiG-15

---

[58] George Air Force Base (1941–1992) is a former United States Air Force base located within city limits, 8 miles northwest of central Victorville, California, about 75 miles northeast of Los Angeles, California. The facility was closed by the Base Realignment and Closure (or BRAC) 1992 commission at the end of the Cold War. It is now the site of Southern California Logistics Airport.

carried two 23-mm and one 37-mm cannon and was designed to destroy enemy bombers.

The MiG's cannons fired heavy, destructive shells at a slow rate while the Sabre's guns fired lighter shells at a much higher rate of fire. In the high-speed dogfights, typical of MiG Alley, communist pilots found it very difficult to hit the F-86s they faced.

On the other hand, Sabre pilots frequently inflicted only light damage because their machine guns lacked the punch of cannons. MiG pilots could then escape across the Yalu River into the safety of Manchuria (although F-86 pilots sometimes followed them in 'hot pursuit').[59]

Browning M-3 Machine Gun
Bore: .50-cal. (12.7 mm)
Muzzle velocity: 2,870 feet per second
Rate of fire: 1,250 rounds per minute
Bullet weight: 1.7 ounces (49 grams)
Gun weight: 65 pounds

Nudelman-Suranov NS-23 Cannon
Bore: 23 mm
Muzzle velocity: 2,250-2,330 feet per second
Rate of fire: 550 rounds per minute
Bullet weight: 6.2 ounces (175 grams)
Gun weight: 81 pounds

Nudelman N-37 Cannon
Bore: 37 mm
Muzzle velocity: 2,260 feet per second

---

[59] (F-86 Sabre vs. MiG-15 Armament)

Rate of fire: 400-450 rounds per minute
Bullet weight: 27 ounces or 1.7 pounds (760 grams)
Gun weight: 227 pounds

The time that they spent together, crunching the numbers and testing tactics, was the dawn of an era in Ralph's life, fostering a life-long bond between himself and Boots. Both men were laid to rest just 37 days apart, 70 years later. They were two American war heroes, and shall never be forgotten.

Boots was one of the greatest aces of the Korean-War era. A graduate of the United States Military Academy in 1945, he flew two combat tours during the Korean War, completing 67 missions in P-51s, 35 missions in F-80s and 121 missions in F-86s. During his second tour in F-86s, he was officially credited with shooting down nine MiG-15s and one La-9. At the time of his return to the United States in October 1952, he was America's leading jet ace.

Blesse remained with fighter aircraft for practically his entire military career. During the 1955 Air Force Worldwide Gunnery Championship, he won all six trophies offered for individual performance, a feat never equaled. During the Vietnam War, he served two tours in Southeast Asia; while on his first tour in 1967-1968, he flew 156 combat missions.

He retired from the United States Air Force in 1975 as a major general, with more than 6,500 flying hours in fighter aircraft and more than 650 hours combat time to his credit.[60]

---

[60] (Master Fighter Tactician: Frederick 'Boots' Blesse)

'Boots' Blesse in his F-86 cockpit. (USAF Photo)

From a pilot's perspective, understanding tactics is your key to survival. You must engrain into your mind to never underestimate the talent of the enemy you're facing. Never provide your opponent a break, and then end the engagement as soon as possible. If you start playing with the enemy because you think you're a better pilot, the next thing you know, one of his buddies has capitalized on your diverted attention and will kill you. Ralph employed that strategy throughout five combat tours in three wars and said that it saved his bacon on numerous occasions.

F-86

Boots and Ralph worked on their F-86 tactics project for nearly a year. There was an immense amount of sweat and fatigue from in-depth preflight planning, flying the missions, then post-flight debriefings. They would discuss the 'what ifs', including discussions on even more improved tactics they still wanted to test. Their squadron mates laughed at them and their lean-forward attitudes, but 'Boots' and Ralph had a burning desire to return to Korea as even more improved fighter pilots but this time in the air-to-air combat regime.

Only one other guy from the squadron showed interest in their efforts and that was Captain Joseph McConnell, Jr. Ralph liked him and talked to Boots about taking him under their wing. They would teach him their newly refined tactics, including aircraft energy management and a multitude of other techniques they were employing.

The eventual top jet ace of the Korean War, McConnell scored his first victory on 14 January 1953. In just over a month, he gained his fifth MiG-15 victory, thereby also becoming an ace.

Capt. Joseph McConnell Jr. in the cockpit of his F-86 aircraft Beauteous Butch II. McConnell became the top US ace in the Korean War. Note the 16 'kill' stars on the fuselage. (USAF photo)

On the day McConnell shot down his eighth MiG, his F-86 was hit by enemy aircraft fire from Russian Ace, Semen Alexeivich Fedoret's MiG-15, and he was forced to bail out over enemy-controlled waters of the Yellow Sea, west of Korea. The impressive war career of Fedorets, a Russian *Asov*, included 98 missions, 8 aerial victories (all F-86E/Fs), being downed once, and being awarded with Lenin's Order—the second highest Soviet military decoration.

While watching the huge air battle from above in his MiG-15bis *Fagot* '93', Fedorets heard one of his comrades crying for help, as he recounted:

"Suddenly, I heard on the radio the anguished voice of one of our pilots crying for help. 'Help me! I got hit!' I

looked down, and I saw, on the right at 90 degrees and 1,500-2,000 meters below, a MiG-15 leaving a black smoke trail, going northwards, pursued by a Sabre which fired at him all the time. I didn't think twice and sharply broke right and descended, getting closer to the Sabre. I gave it two bursts at 100-300 meters. After the second one, the Sabre lost control, turned to the right and dove to the ground."

The pilot of that F-86E probably was Norman E. Green, a young pilot of the 335th FIS, who ejected and was rescued. However, as Fedorets was shooting down Green, a flight of four Sabres of the 39th FIS was closing in from behind. Even when Fedorets didn't know it then, that flight was led by an ace with 7 MiG kills in his score and future leading American Ace of the Korean conflict, Captain Joseph McConnell:

My #3 and #4, Aleksandrov and Shorin, lost track of me during my sharp maneuvers, but my wingman, V. Yefremov, stayed with me. When I was closing to the Sabre, I heard Yefremov saying: 'A flight of Sabres behind.' He radioed such info, and he went away to the left, leaving me alone without cover. As soon as I stopped looking through the gunsight and I turned my head, a short burst struck my cockpit from the right and above.

"I sharply broke to the right, underneath the Sabre, getting out of the line of fire. The Sabre went forward and ended up in front of me at my right. The American pilot turned his head, he saw me and engaged flaps, with the intent to slow down, to let me pass forward and to riddle me at short range. I realized his maneuver and

sharply broke left, while firing a burst at the Sabre without aiming. The burst struck the base of the right wing, close to the fuselage. A huge hole, about one square meter, appeared in the wing of the Sabre. It broke to the right and fell downwards. That was my second enemy aircraft destroyed in that combat."

Fedorets was right in one thing: McConnell's Sabre was mortally wounded. But what Fedorets didn't know then was that, even with his F-86F badly shot-up, McConnell still could perform a barrel-roll which put him at 6 o'clock of the now unaware Fedorets. And then, he took revenge for his defeat.

"As soon as I got my plane out of the attack, from below, I was hit by a machine gun burst. I sharply pushed the stick and tried to disengage. The cockpit was filled with smoke and kerosene, the instrument panel was destroyed, and finally, the new couple of Sabres [Fedorets did not know then that it was the same Sabre piloted by McConnell that he had knocked out before.] *broke any control. Using the trimmer, I leveled the plane and decided to bail out. With a tremendous effort, I was able to eject the canopy and successfully bailed out of my damaged plane at 11,000 meters of altitude."*

However, the hunter did not survive his prey for much longer. McConnell ejected out of his badly damaged F-86F over the East China Sea and was immediately picked up by an H-19 rescue helicopter. Certainly, a Clash of Titans happened that day: one excellent Russian Ace knocked out an American Ace and made him his 6th kill, but before bailing out, this American Ace (future top American scorer of the war) transformed his Russian defeater into his 8th victory. A Hollywood director could not have written a better script. That single combat legend today is a proof of the top class of the pilots who fought each other over North Korea years ago.

That day ended up with a tied match: four MiGs downed by Sabres—2 Russians, 2 Chinese—but also four American fighters were lost due to Russian MiG-15 *Fagots*: besides Fedorets bagging the F-86s of Green and McConnell, *Starsii Leiutenant* Grigorii Berelidze (224th IAP) had shot down 1st Lt. Robert Niemann's F-86E (MIA); finally, another pilot of the 913th IAP, *Kapetan* Semenov, scored one F-84E down (James Wills, KIA).[61]

After only two minutes in the freezing water, McConnell was rescued via helicopter. The following day, he was back in combat and shot down his ninth MiG. By the end of April 1953, he had scored his 10th victory to become a double ace.

He scored his last victories on May 18, 1953. That morning, McConnell shot down two MiGs in a furious air battle and became a triple ace with 15 kills. On another mission that afternoon, he shot down his 16th and final MiG-15.

On August 25, 1954, McConnell crashed to his death while testing an F-86H at Edwards AFB, Calif.[62] McConnell AFB was aptly named after this true American hero and is home of the Air Force's 22nd Air Refueling Wing in Wichita, KS.

---

[61] (Zampini and Sherman)

[62] (Leading Jet Ace: Capt. Joseph McConnell, Jr.)

As their testing progressed, the top brass started to listen to what Parr and Blesse had to say. Most of them were strictly prop-oriented pilots from the earlier days, having made their mark in P-51s and P-47s. They probably thought, *What could a couple of squadron-level pilots in the lower echelons possibly know about flying combat and pushing the F-86 to its maximum capability?* But 'Boots' and Ralph's legacy was born.

During that project, they discovered the importance of speed. Speed always provides a distinct advantage. With speed, you could obtain the element of surprise, and with surprise, you would find many of your ground targets still relatively motionless. If the enemy knew that you were coming, the ground targets were guaranteed to be on the move, making target acquisition much more difficult. The new Sabre jets provided a decent advantage when it came to speed and surprise.[63]

Ralph was assigned to take part in F-86D rocket firing and accuracy tests. He went on temporary duty (TDY) for two to three months to the North American factory in California to do work with the test engineers at Mojave. They would spend their nights in Los Angeles and fly up to Mojave on the shuttle the first thing in the morning, then returning home on the shuttle each evening. The F-86D rocket tests involved five-inch, unguided High-Velocity Aircraft Rockets, or 'Hi-VARs', also nicknamed Holy Moses. The tests were unsuccessful as the results revealed that the rockets weren't feasible for use on the F-86D as a firing platform. The test

---

[63] (R. S. Parr, personal interview)

managers were employing Ralph's air-to-air gunnery knowledge for their input.

As other testing continued, it was determined that the short range or 'legs' of the new fighter was problematic but not insurmountable. Minimal onboard fuel capacity limited loiter time near the target, depending on your distance between your base and the target area.

Added tanks for added range—A line of F-86 Sabrejets of the 4th Fighter-Interceptor Wing in Korea await attachment of wing tanks which will give them longer cruising range in their flights over North Korea in quest of MiGs. When Sabre jet pilots sight the MiGs, they release their wing tanks, thereby gaining speed as they move to engage the enemy pilots.

A young officer named Johnson came up with a magnificent idea to nearly double the size of the F-86 wing tip fuel tank, vastly increasing loiter time. Additional loiter time saved countless lives when flying close-air support sorties for American infantry. The infantry had become accustomed to enjoying the air force ground support efforts. Casualties would mount if those airborne assets rendered unavailable, thus creating gaps in support coverage due to original fuel limitations.[64]

As the MiG-15 numbers increased in theatre, the U.S. deployed the 4th Fighter Wing with their new North American F-86 Sabres, to counter this threat. This began the long series of F-86 vs. MiG-15 battles in the notorious MiG Alley near the Yalu River.[65]

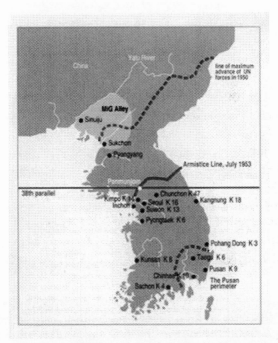

MiG Alley (Smithsonian Air & Space Museum)

Rising losses of B-29s and their aircrews drew the attention of everyone at the Pentagon but none more than

---

[64] (R. S. Parr, personal interview)

[65] (Thompson)

General Vandenberg[66] who sought answers to how to better protect our bombers. The climax was during a mission on 23 October, dubbed 'Black Tuesday', lives in the memory of B-29 crews as their darkest day of the Korean War. Eight B-29s from the 307th BG (of nine that began the mission) went forth to bomb Namsi airfield at Sinuiju, along the Yalu. The weather was supposed to be clear and, sadly, it was. The day began when Sabres downed two MiGs near the Yalu but subsequently withdrew before an escort of Thunderjets proved unable to protect their bomber charges.

MiGs caught the B-29s over their target, the size of the communist fighter force having been variously estimated at somewhere between 55 and 150. Three B-29s were shot down, and all but one of the surviving bombers received major damage. A number of these were carrying dead and wounded crewmen aboard when they made emergency landings in Japan and Korea. Only one B-29 (44-87760) returned safely to its base. The F-84s scored one MiG kill, which was credited to navy exchange pilot Lt (later CAPT) Walter Schirra, who later became a Mercury and Apollo astronaut, but the Thunderjets also lost one of their own.

B-29 gunners were credited with the destruction of a MiG-15, but the Soviet jets pressed their attacks home and shot down a bomber over Wonsan harbor.

---

[66] Gen. Hoyt S. Vandenberg (1899-1954) served as the U.S. Air Force chief of staff during the Korean War. He was promoted to full general in 1948, becoming the youngest four-star officer in the U.S. armed forces.

Three days later, again with Meteor and Thunderjet escorts, Superfortresses returned to the bridge at Sinuiju. The approach to the target was made over the Yellow Sea in the belief (correct, as it turned out) that MiG pilots would not fight over water since their air force had no apparatus to rescue a pilot downed at sea. The Superfortresses encountered MiGs only after making landfall, but the fighting was furious. One bomber gunner was credited with a MiG and a B-29 was severely damaged.

On 28 October, the final day of sustained daytime B-29 operations in the face of the MiG threat, the 98th Bomb Group sent eight Superfortresses to strike a bridge at Sunchon. MiGs were seen in the area but they did not engage the bombers. During the month of October, FEAF had lost seven F-86s, five Superfortresses, two Thunderjets, and an RF-80 in battle. The five B-29s almost equaled the previous figure of six lost in the entire war. Alarmed at these losses, General Vandenberg made a quick trip to the region, where he received discouraging reports from B-29 crewmembers.

'Mac' McGill remembers the general's visit well; the pilot stepping down from his bomber after an uneventful mission to learn that Vandenberg had just flown in from the Pentagon.

Staff officers swarmed around the chief of staff, anxious to hand him briefing papers. A colonel wanted to hand him a memorandum to study. "Get rid of that stuff," Vandenberg snapped. "I want to talk to the tail gunner. I want B-29 crew members around me here. I don't want to talk to anyone else." According to McGill, bomber crews told Vandenberg that their 0.50-cal machine guns were just about useless. The general asked a member of McGill's crew about the armament. "It's worthless," the man replied. "Anything would be better than what we've got." An air force sergeant pointed out that several of the men were officially credited with shooting down MiGs, but none seriously believed they had really done so. Today, the best evidence is that they were right.

When Vandenberg returned to Washington D.C., he was considering the prospect that the United States might have to withdraw its B-29s from the Korean theatre entirely. Curiously enough, however, there is no evidence that anyone suggested replacing the B-29s with newer B-50's. It remains unclear, even today, why the B-50—which flew reconnaissance missions in the combat zone—was never used as a bomber in the Korean War. In the end, the only decision made was one to strengthen the F-86 force, but the enemy was increasing its fighter arsenal, too.

By the end of 1951, a handful of MiGs had been moved to the North Korean side of the Yalu, and the MiG-15b model, with its improved engine, was being introduced into the combat zone. For a brief period, it appeared that the Soviets—whom the Americans steadfastly believed were Chinese—intended to extend their airpower to the battle lines and beyond. On at least one occasion, MiGs ventured south of Seoul, which was now in UN hands. Weyland reported to his superiors that there was a 'serious danger' of the enemy challenging US air superiority. Briefly, Tupolev Tu-2 bombers were also seen, and engaged, along the Yalu.

The MiG threat to the B-29 force was one reason why Vandenberg and the Pentagon brass reversed their long-standing policy and agreed to move a second fighter wing of F-86s to Korea. By the end of 1951, the 51st FIW had joined the 4th in patrolling 'MiG Alley'.[67]

By late spring 1951, the lines had stabilized, and a battle of position began that would last another 27 months. By now, the opposing ground forces were well dug in, and neither side could gain much ground and hold it. The Chinese held the edge in manpower, and the United Nations' forces held the edge in firepower. This situation could change only if the enemy were able to accumulate enough supplies to initiate a substantial offensive. With this in mind, United Nations' airpower continued to destroy anything that moved southward. The spectacular aerial duels between the F-86 and MiG-15 continued, for it was essential for UN forces to maintain air superiority, allowing their bombers and fighter-bombers to operate almost with impunity.[68]

Ralph was chomping at the bit to get back to Korea for a second tour; now using the new F-86 Sabre. During that time, a pilot couldn't return for a second tour until everyone else had been deployed for at least their first tour. There were enough people trying to find loop holes or other jobs to keep from going at all. Only five or six pilots actually returned for a second tour. Boots and Ralph worked every possible angle in order to be selected for a second tour. In the end, one guy's father was a brigadier general which helped their situation during the decision process. Boots departed for his second tour ahead of Ralph.

---

[67] (Varhola)

[68] (Thompson)

When Ralph finally was selected to go back to Korea for a second tour, he not only wanted to go back to test their newly developed tactics and theories, but he really wanted to fly air-to-air combat missions, since his first tour was primarily air-to-ground. Then, there were no real air-to-air opportunities while flying the F-80.

Near the end of April, Ralph was sitting at Camp Stoneman in Antioch, California, reading large headlines that the war was ending soon. Now, he was slated to head back to Korea on a boat, which would make his deployment trip a couple of weeks long. He decided to expend all the energy that he had on garnering air transportation to speed up the deployment process. He finally found a transport airplane headed for Japan, and with all of the logistics arrangements in place, he had orders to report to the 4th Fighter-Interceptor Wing.

He hopped on an old C-124 Globe master and lumbered across the Pacific. While speeding over the top of numerous ships, he smiled and thought, *Oh, how things could have been much different*, thankful that he wasn't one of those ship passengers below. After the aircraft landed, he rode a bus over to wing headquarters. There, at Kimpo AB, he ran into Maj. Steve Bettinger, whom he'd been stationed with on a previous assignment.

Bettinger asked, "What are you doing over here? You've already been here for a tour."

Ralph replied, "I've come back to fly air-to-air missions in the 335th Fighter-Interceptor Squadron in the 4th Fighter-Interceptor Wing and I'm damn glad to be here."

Colonel James K. Johnson was the commander at the time. Although truce negotiations were in the initial stages, Ralph didn't want the door to flying air-to-air combat missions slammed in his face before he launched on his first sortie. He flew about seven weeks' worth of air-to-air combat missions before the armistice was signed. The 335th Fighter-Interceptor Squadron came away from Korea with 218.5 confirmed combat kills, topping its sister squadrons by a considerable margin.

Competition among the squadrons during that time was very high. They didn't interact with each other much. Even the squadron heads knew only about half the people in the other squadrons. They were fighting like hell to maintain the elite status of their own squadron, but they didn't let any outsiders in to attack another unit. They were all one team, a family. The feeling throughout all squadrons was, "We can mess with our own brothers and sisters, but don't you dare mess with them or I'll take your ass out!"[69]

It was normal to have squadron colors and emblems that accompanied each unit patch and members of each squadron displayed them proudly. There were the 'Fighting Eagles', the 'Chiefs', and the 'Rocketeers'.

Most of the intra-squadron rivalries went much deeper than simply the pilot side of the house. Crew chiefs and supply guys were involved too. They were betting cases of beer on whose pilots would come back with the most kills the next day.

Ralph mentioned to the crew chief one day, "Boy, you're doing an outstanding job keeping my airplane in

---

[69] (R. S. Parr, personal interview)

commission so it's ready to go when I'm ready to fly." It hadn't once gone out of commission due to maintenance issues or lack of parts, once.

He replied, "Well, you know why that is, don't you, sir?"

Ralph said, "No, I just figured you were doing an outstanding job."

He said, "Yeah, but it's easy because the supply guys are almost six months ahead on cases of beer by betting on you. I'm not about to let your airplane go out of commission because of parts."

A smile crept across Ralph's face as the crew chief earned a gentlemanly pat on the back. "Keep up the great work," Ralph replied.

The pilots were self-motivated. No single outfit possessed all highly motivated pilots. Those who espoused to the theory that one squadron was simply loaded with talent was simply blowing wind. You would find some pilots were reluctant to fly for one reason or another, while others weren't afraid to fly at all. In order to know which were which, you'd get down in the middle of the pilots at gatherings and through five minutes of conversation, you'd quickly figure out who was afraid to accept the risks and needed an extra dose of intestinal fortitude.

The normal Korean War pilot tour was limited to 100 missions, but that could be waived or extended to 125 missions if required. Colonel Vermont Garrison, the 335th Fighter-Interceptor Commander in 1953, made one of the biggest miscalculations of the war. On June 1, 1953, during the 04:00 briefing, he stated that he would buy steaks and drinks for any pilot logging confirmed

MiG kills during the month. The bad part for him was that he made that statement before Ralph got his first kill and he'd never heard about the wager.

Colonel Garrison was an absolutely superior combat leader, particularly while airborne. He was very laid back; nothing really got to him or rattled him. From a management perspective, Ralph wasn't privy to how he handled the administrative end of the squadron but felt that he owed Garrison a lot for enabling Ralph to fly as often as he did. Had Garrison not put in a good word for Ralph, he would have still been waiting to become mission ready.

There's a difference between managers and leaders. You can't really train leaders like some people think. Managers sometimes don't make good leaders. A combat leader possesses a compilation of varying skill sets rolled into one, with a fair amount of experience and background from which to draw. But Garrison was a damn good leader, and so was Jimmy Johnson (Col. James K. Johnson), the 4th Fighter Wing Commander.

The 4th Fighter-Interceptor Wing began the Korean War with F-86As and then transitioned to F-86Es as the conflict continued. The modification Ralph remembered most was the irreversible controls implemented in the F-86E models, which provided power-boosted controls. Then in the 'F' model, engineers made a few more refinements, including an improved gun sight and 'six-three' leading edges, which provided a hard-leading edge on the wing.

The regular 'F' model had automatic slats on each side, but they retrofitted the wings six inches forward at the wing root and three inches (hence the name 'six-three') forward at the wing tip, providing a larger wing surface and enabling the pilot to maintain your speed in a turn, even at altitude. There no longer were automatic slats that extended, creating drag and bleeding off energy in a high-G turn.

The F-86 played a crucial role and was the mainstay during the Korean War. Although airpower could not win the Korean War for the United Nations, it did neutralize the communist forces and force the community leadership to enter an armistice. On 10 July 1951, truce negotiations began at Kaesong. They were moved over to Panmunjom on 12 November 1951, where they would remain until the war ended. For the first few months, there were high hopes that the war would end soon, but these meeting would continue on and off for the next two years.[70]

---

[70] (Thompson)

Chapter 8
Dirty Guns

Today was the 11th anniversary of the end of the WWII Battle of Midway, a key United States' naval victory in the Pacific. Not realizing that fact, an anxious yet confident Ralph awoke early that sunny Sunday morning, feeling extremely rested and ready to fly. Never feeling fearful or apprehensive about flying and fighting, the thought of the unknown or what lies ahead during today's sortie always hung in the back of Ralph's overly focused mind. It was 7 June 1953, and he was extremely eager and excited to fly his F-86 in the number four position of a four-ship formation that day.

The briefing went off without a hitch with 1st Lt. Mervin Ricker as lead, Colonel Robert J. Dixon was number two, 2nd Lt. Al Cox was number three, and Ralph was number four.

The mission was fragged, as most were at that time, as a fighter sweep in hopes of finding enemy aircraft lurking around up in 'MiG Alley'.

MiG Alley is the name construed by American pilots
for the far northwest portion of North Korea. It was easy
to spot from the air as it was the airspace above the Yalu
River, the defining border between North Korea and
China. The airspace, normally saturated with MiGs,
stretched from Sinuiju at the southwest end where the
Yalu River dumps into the Yellow Sea to the Kanggye at
the northeast end of the airspace. Although Ralph arrived
late to the fight, about seven weeks from the end of the
conflict, he piggy-backed on his predecessors' claim that
MiG Alley was the birthplace of jet fighter combat.[71]

Following the sortie briefing, Ralph and the three
others stopped by the life support shop to gather their
flight gear, including helmets, parachutes, and other pro

[71] (R. S. Parr, personal interview)

gear before their walk out to the aircraft. With about 50 yards of their journey complete, a semi-somber Al Cox turned to Ralph and said, "You know, you've got more F-86 time than I have total flight time and I know it's not what the books say, but if you see something out there, call it out. If I don't see it right away, I'll clear you to take the bounce (a fighter pilot term meaning unexpected attack on another aircraft) and I'll cover you." This would cause a role reversal as Ralph flying as number four should have been the 'looker' for Al, who was the 'shooter' flying as number three in the formation.

Ralph grinned and replied, "It sounds like a good idea to me."

They arrived at the four fully armed and fueled aircraft to peruse the maintenance forms with their respective crew chiefs, performed their walk arounds, and interior preflight checklists. They started engines, taxied and took off on time climbing out towards MiG Alley, eventually leveling off at 43,000 feet.

As they entered the area heading northeasterly and paralleling the Yalu River, off their left wing, Ralph immediately spotted four fast-moving aircraft flying southwest (opposite direction) at a very low altitude. He just happened to look down and caught a sudden glimmer of sunlight reflecting off a fast-moving fighter's canopy or a wing against the darker, tree-covered ground.

Not knowing the aircraft type, Ralph immediately pressed the mic button and called the traffic out to his wingman, "I've got a bogie low, real low at 2 o'clock, opposite direction."

Al immediately replied, "I don't have him; you take him, I've got you covered."

Ralph grabbed the stick and started a half roll, letting the nose slice through the horizon and sending his aircraft into a split-S. Trading altitude for airspeed, his Sabre's airspeed indicator spun like a top as he now screamed toward the ground, with thicker air found at lower altitudes its only resistance. He was heading straight down from 43,000 feet, throttle wide open with his airspeed increasing exponentially with each second that passed. He rolled out on a heading that he thought was at or near the same direction he had seen the reflection heading just seconds earlier.

Cox called out over the radio, "Which way did you go?"

Ralph quickly replied, "I'm headed straight down, come down and try to find me."

Now Ralph recognized that he was passing through 10,000 feet and remembered Air Force F-86 tech data stated that if heading straight down, it takes 7.33 Gs and 14,500 ft. of altitude to safely pull out of a dive without augering straight into the ground. Somewhat surprised, Ralph found himself screaming through 10,000 feet and knew that he needed more than 7.33 Gs to safely pull out of this dive. He yanked hard on the stick, initiating his pullout with eight Gs.

It only took a split-second for him to realize that the ground was not yet passing 'that fast' underneath him, so he increased his pull with both hands on the stick, pulling as hard as he could, pinning it against the aft stop. As the aircraft went to 9 Gs, his G-suit was now fully inflated, squeezing tightly on his legs and abdomen, his body felt like it weighed over 1,600 lbs, he knew it was going to be close. He thought he'd either make it or stick his aircraft straight into the ground. He glanced at the ejection handles as he still had the stick pulled against the aft stop, frantically contemplating whether he should eject or ride it out to see what happens. He was also afraid that his wings may fail due to his blistering airspeed. It was going to be real close. The aircraft was flying like a bat out of hell when he finally pulled out at the bottom of his dive, leveling at 300 feet above ground level (AGL).

He gathered his wits and caught his breath. A couple of hard blinks and a quick head shake enabled his eyes to refocus as he scanned forward and spotted two MiG-15s. He adjusted his heading a few degrees and started tracking them. He was now at idle with his speed brakes deployed patiently awaiting the effects of the reduced thrust and increased drag to slow him down. His huge overtake in airspeed continued on the flight of MiGs even as his aircraft continued slowing rapidly.

Then he saw that the two MiGs that he was tracking had others in their flight. Those two turned into four, and the four turned into eight. There were two flights of four, totaling eight aircraft. The sudden increase in MiG to Sabre ratio startled Ralph as he thought, *God, keep your eyes open.* He snatched looks out either side of the canopy and noticed another eight MiGs on his right, flying parallel to his course. Now a total of 16 adversaries wanted a piece of him.[72]

The eight MiGs that he was chasing had broken formation and headed in all directions except down. All were still below 500 feet. He started tracking the leader. Ralph chose him because he figured that pilot would be

---

[72] (R. S. Parr, personal interview)

the best and most experienced, or he wouldn't be leading. Ralph wanted to take the leader out before he took on the wingmen[73]. He continued tracking the lead aircraft. The war was about to end and this engagement may be his only chance of seeing any similar air-to-air action, so he broke formation with the lead pilot, frantically fighting to maintain position.

Ralph planned his turn, placing his aircraft on the inside of the turn to cut the corner, but still couldn't close the gap on him. Ralph was at 9.5 Gs and the enemy now adjusted his airspeed, sucking Ralph in even closer. Ralph was trying everything possible to drop back into a tracking position for a good shot. Ralph went to idle, attempting to slide back into firing position but knew that he didn't want to 'give away' airspeed, too. He didn't realize then, but this mission reconstruction would later turn into a full-fledged classroom lesson on aircraft energy management.

As the two aircraft approached similar airspeeds, Ralph began to feed in the power and pulled his speed brakes in. He couldn't continue to hold the high G load as he could feel the aircraft trembling with the onslaught of a high-speed stall. The time was now! He 'leaned' on the trigger and got a half dozen to 10 hits along the length of the enemy's fuselage. That forced the MiG to pull up to gain some altitude, which is exactly what Ralph anticipated. Ralph stuck right with him and dished outside to slow down his overtake, which was now considerably reduced. Each aircraft was racing at over

---

[73] Ralph remembered, "Their break was wild. It looked like parts of a soft banana being fed through a high speed fan."

350 knots; Ralph slowly passed the MiG, pulled even harder, attempting to 'suck' his enemy around the turn. Ralph had to do something quick, so he pulled his aircraft up and rolled inverted, sliding in high on the MiG, canopy to canopy and at the same airspeed.

Col. Parr holds models of his F-86 (top) and MiG-15, depicting his position when he rolled his streaking jet up over on top of the MiG-15 adversary.

Years later, Ralph was in Las Vegas at Nellis AFB, discussing our air-to-air capabilities during the war in Korea. He was in a hangar, putting on a pitch for the F-86 pilots. When he finished his portion of the discussion, a movie producer came over to visit with him. He had overheard Ralph's discussion of his canopy-to-canopy encounter with the MiG-15 and found it intriguing. He asked Ralph if he minded if they incorporated that scene into a movie that they were working on. They didn't have a name for the movie at that time. Ralph told him that he didn't mind at all if they used that scenario for their movie . . . the rest is history. When Ralph saw *Top Gun*, he said, "Hey, I've been there before!"

During his days at Nellis AFB, Ralph worked a lot with 'Boots' Blesse on defining many basic fighter maneuvers that would help gain an advantage over the enemy in a dogfight. They worked on numerous maneuvers to gain any advantage. After 'Boots' made ace, he came back to Nellis to pass his info on to the other pilots. 'Boots' stayed there and wrote the book *'No Guts No Glory'*, which was used as a pilot handbook on the subject. The message in his book saved countless American lives.

The cover of 'No Guts No Glory!'
By 'Boots' Blesse[74]

Ralph had no idea that lessons from his current situation would be included in Blesse's book.

After momentarily looking down into the MiG's cockpit, Ralph had to try something else to gain the edge while maneuvering his aircraft into firing position. He retarded the throttle, attempting to creep back on him. Knowing that the thicker air at lower altitudes helped your turn rate, he yanked hard on the stick, entering a high-G turn. The enemy saw Ralph slide out and decelerate to improve position, so he countered by turning into Ralph at a hilariously low altitude. They were so low.

---

[74] A PDF version of 'No Guts No Glory!' is available online.

Ralph thought to himself, *Jesus Christ! I can see the leaves on the trees.*

Ralph slid back even further, easing himself into the saddle (at the enemy's 6 o'clock and in firing position). At about the same time, the MiG rolled under, and Ralph went with him. When he rolled out, Ralph thought, *We're too goddamned low to be doing this. All I need to do is put one wingtip into his jet wash and I'm gone.* Ralph didn't want to do that maneuver again.[75]

The MiG quickly reversed his turn and did another roll in the opposite direction; this time Ralph went up over the top of him, gaining about 20 feet, and again he leaned on the trigger. Ralph wound up in the saddle, holding 9.5 Gs to maintain position on him, then his day took a turn for the worse.

The overly aggressive maneuver blew Ralph's gunsight fuse, forcing him to fly the remainder of the mission without an active gunsight. He didn't know what caused it, but later learned that he had 'over G'd' the airplane, forcing the gunsight fuse to blow. He had noticed that the rate of fire had started to slow when he scored those initial 6 to 10 hits on the MiG. Apparently, the immense and sustained G-load was too much for the electric motors that now were no longer lifting the .50-caliber ammunition through the magazines to feed the guns. He knew that he had to momentarily release the trigger. As Ralph slid back behind the MiG, he pulled the nose up and hosed him to ribbons, forcing him to go straight into the ground.

---

[75] (R. S. Parr, personal interview)

A relieved yet elated Ralph had logged his first kill but knew that he didn't want to mess with that guy again.

A team of Russian Generals came to the United States after the Korean War on a fact-finding mission. There were four retired Russian Generals seeking information concerning their MIAs during the Korean War. They had a list of names and they were trying to find out the circumstances regarding their missing comrades.

The head of the Russian delegation carried the list and showed it to Ralph. It wasn't the name on the list that meant anything to him, but Ralph recognized the sortie information that they carried concerning their missing pilot on his final mission. Ralph recognized an instance on one of the pages as his own first aerial kill, on his first F-86 mission that he flew in Korea. The details that they carried concerning the mission were unbelievably accurate.

The Russian General sat down with Ralph, scouring the information. The first one on his list matched perfectly in the date, time of day, and the area; all were identical with Ralph's first mission. No others on their list matched up with any of Ralph's other sorties, however, it was obvious that the fight in question was his kill.

Ralph was well aware of the fact that this pilot's abilities nearly matched those of our best American pilots and he realized that during the initial portion of the attack. The Russians had lost one of their best, which is what drove the general's pointed questions regarding that sortie.

Ralph had never eaten flames and debris like he did on that particular mission. He had raced through enormous flames that licked at his canopy like dragon fire and large pieces of MiG debris as it disintegrated in midair. Ralph carried that visual in his head until the day he died.

Ralph headed back to the base. When he landed and stepped down from his jet, everyone on the ground stood in awe. There were soot tenders all over Ralph's aircraft. It looked like someone had gone over portions of his airplane with a blow torch at close range. All his life, he had strived to fly fighters in combat, and who would have known that he'd experience it on his first air-to-air combat duty day.

He knew that this is what he'd worked so hard to attain. He was loving life.[76]

Ralph had just had his way with one MiG (his first kill) and was about to relax for a moment to gather himself together.[77]

About that time, a MiG-15 went over the top of him with his guns thumping. Ralph looked to his right and saw five of them, all lined up, ready to take their best run at him. They weren't happy that he had just shot down their flight lead.

The first of five rolled in on him, and he could hear the MiG's guns blazing. Then the second one started, and he could hear his rattling guns even louder than the first. All five made identical passes at him. Just before the fifth

---

[76] (R. S. Parr, personal interview)

[77] Ralph remembered, "I thought: '*look around, you idiot, there are others up here!*'"

one started firing, the first one stopped firing, and the aircraft overshot him. Ralph had too much turn on him. Then the second one overshot him too. At the time, it looked like all their firepower was going over top his tail, but they were actually going beneath him. Ralph achieved more spacing after they overshot him, and then another MiG took a shot that went over his canopy by three or four aircraft lengths. Ralph looked back, and number five was breaking off his engagement.

Ralph figured that the fifth MiG thought he wasn't going to be able to hack the turn just like his wingmen. Ralph slacked off his pull, reducing the G-load. He knew that he didn't have an active gunsight, so reducing the G-load allowed his guns to work properly. He pushed up the power, increasing his closure rate, which made the MiG pilot climb away from him. That enabled Ralph to pull right up behind the MiG and hose him with a steady stream of gunfire. The MiG immediately burst into flames and cart wheeled in.

Ralph wasn't sure what had happened to the original eight MiGs capping the dogfight, but Al Cox watched the furball from above and during the debrief, Cox said, "There were eight MiGs capping the fight. The other eight MiGs and Parr were dancing together at very low altitude." Laughter filled the room.

'Shooter's Odds'

**Colonel Parr holds his double aces with Ross Buckland's
painting, 'Shooter's Odds' in the background.**

Ralph narrowly escaped death after rolling his
aircraft into a Split-S, forcing his F-86F straight down
from 43,000 feet and closed rapidly on the suspicious
image. Soon, he saw four MiG-15s in front of him, but a
quick look left and right revealed a total of 16 enemy
aircraft. Not one to miss an opportunity, Parr engaged the
closest aircraft and was immediately in a boiling dogfight
right on the deck. Note the speed breaks deployed on
lower aft fuselage and the red stripe on Ralph's helmet
seen in the cockpit.

Ralph ended up killing two out of the initial eight and
damaged one. The remaining six MiGs and the capping
eight all bugged out and headed home to the northwest

over the Yalu River. They'd either seen enough or were low on fuel.

Ralph's good South Carolina friend and wingman, Al Cox, was killed in a mid-air collision two weeks later. Ralph was lead, and Al was sitting right on Ralph's wing, flying fat, dumb, and happy when number three in the flight hit Al in mid-air. Unable to bail out, both pilots rode their aircraft in and perished.

One day, the crew chief and Ralph painted Ralph's name on the rail below the canopy on his F-86. Ralph had his helmet there at the aircraft, and he figured, "Hell, I'm in the 'chief's' squadron, so I'll do something to enhance the morale of my crew chief." He took a piece of red masking tape and cut a straight line on one end and then ran it over the top of his helmet right down the center. Ralph told him, "This will be my scalp lock."

Col. Parr's flight helmet, including its red stripe sitting atop the casket at his interment.

The crew chief said, "Why put it on the helmet?"

Ralph said, "The helmet is the only thing that shows from the cockpit. If more than one enemy sees it and he

145

safely makes it back to his base, he'll report that he fought the guy with a red stripe on his helmet to his intel folks in debrief. Should that happen two or three times, it could induce a distraction or draw their focus to something else during the fight."

Ralph was willing to do anything to gain a psychological edge on his next adversary. Ralph wanted that MiG pilot to think, "Uh oh, what have we here?" It could drive his attention to the red stripe rather than his next evasive maneuver. The stripe was merely meant to rattle their cage. Ralph's 'red stripe' is depicted in the painting, 'Shooter's Odds' by Ross Buckland.[78]

The squadron insignia at that time was an Indian head with chief feathers. When Ralph got back from that mission, his crew chief said, "Boy, you really scalped 'em." He was cleaning gunpowder residue from Ralph's gun ports and fuselage. He knew that he'd have that task ahead of him as Ralph approached the airfield because when the aircraft returned to base and entered the break for landing, ground crews would look for dark smudges on the wings, which meant that F-86 pilot had fired his guns during the mission. If they saw the smudges, they'd call out 'dirty guns over the radio. That call would bring everyone out to the strip to check you out when you taxied in, each yearning to hear the details of your dogfight. There was no greater feeling than taxiing in with 'dirty guns'.

---

[78] (R. S. Parr, personal interview)

Chapter 9
Against All Odds

Everyone remembers at least one life experience when they faced a situation offering little chance of success. Most can rattle off numerous personal examples with minimal effort and even less time. Venturing back to biblical times, David faced unfathomable odds when forced to go one-on-one against a behemoth opponent in Goliath.[79] To the amazement of all onlookers, David killed a much larger and dominant foe with a single stone slung perfectly into Goliath's forehead. The giant crumbled to the ground in a pool of blood, forehead caved in, and a new hero was born.

Years later, there was the 'Miracle on Ice', the amazing run by the 1980 United States Olympic hockey team, winning a medal round game vs. Russia and then the gold medal vs. Finland. Not only was the Russia game the biggest sports upset of all-time, but this event had an impact on various levels. It was really an overshadowed political event where democracy won out over communism for one night on the ice in a jam-packed stadium in Lake Placid, New York; it also said something

---

[79] The story of David vs. Goliath is found in 1 Samuel 17:1-58 of the Bible.

about the attitude of sportsmen in terms of professionals vs. amateurs.

Even more importantly, *everyone* in the United States shared in this moment. But for one night, people who didn't know a two-line pass from an off-side call were fans of our United States' hockey team. The Cold War overtones of the unstoppable evil Russian empire and its team of professionals who had won eight of the last nine Olympic gold medals vs. the baby-faced kids from the United States, representing all that was good about amateur sports in the Olympics. This was the epitome of a David vs. Goliath story as these two teams didn't even belong on the same sheet of ice.

A third event where man again faced unrelenting odds is nestled in time between those two historic events. MiG Alley would once again welcome Ralph flying in the number three position of a flight of four being led by Colonel Vermont Garrison. They flew together often and Ralph enjoyed the skills Garrison brought to the fight. On this particular sortie like so many before, the element leads (Garrison and Ralph) were the two shooters; the two wingmen were the lookers. They had enjoyed an enormous amount of success flying as a team.

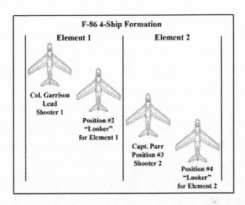

F-86 4-Ship Formation

Element 1   Element 2

Col. Garrison
Lead
Shooter 1

Position #2
"Looker"
for Element 1

Capt. Parr
Position #3
Shooter 2

Position #4
"Looker"
for Element 2

Cruising at 41,000 feet, Garrison's flight had just entered hostile territory, generating a large adrenaline rush in each of the four pilots. Ralph sat straight up in his uncomfortable seat, adjusting his posture behind his cinched restraining straps to improve his circulation as he sought the most comfortable position in the confines of his ejection seat. He split his concentrated focus between maintaining his aircraft position on Garrison's jet in the formation and searching well ahead of the flight for enemy MiGs in the area. That's when he caught a glimpse of the bellies of a large group of MiG-15s making a very gradual turn away and about 2,000 feet below. His quick check of his math confirmed that there were four 4-ships or 16 enemy aircraft below.

Garrison gently lowered the nose of his F-86 and his three wingmen followed in the descent, maintaining position. Garrison changed his flight's heading by 20 or 30 degrees to match the MiGs' heading, then directed the flight to drop their wing tanks to reduce drag while increasing performance. The tail chase was underway. Garrison slowly pushed his stick to the left about the width of a quarter, easing his flight of four into a left turn. Ralph worked extremely hard to stay in position on the right side of the formation while still maintaining visual on Garrison and the adversaries. The left turn threw Ralph's aircraft astern, and he said, "For Christ's sakes, Gary, don't pick the last guy in the MiG formation to shoot . . . pick someone up front so we both can open up on 'em at the same time," because when the first shot is fired, the element of surprise is gone. He knew it would be a bomb burst of MiGs once the shooting began creating a furball of airplanes in the cramped airspace.

Garrison chose the last guy and hosed him pretty well. Obviously shocked, the MiG immediately performed a "Split S" (a flight maneuver including a half roll and inverted dive), and the other 15 enemy airplanes broke to the right. The lead ship of that group broke from formation and performed a wingover maneuver. 'Gary' rolled and continued after the MiG that he had already hit. Ralph didn't realize it at the time, but his own guns had jammed and the leader of the 16-ship pack started to climb on Garrison for a shot. Ralph immediately forgot about the rest of the MiGs and cut the corner off in the turn to catch the MiG on Gary's tail. It was critical for Ralph to get that MiG pilot's mind off Garrison and he was a helluva lot closer to Garrison than Ralph was to the MiG.[80]

About the time the MiG was squared away to fire on Garrison, Ralph pulled hard on the stick, enabling his guns to track through the enemy aircraft's flight path. Knowing that his guns couldn't reach the enemy due to

---

[80] (R. S. Parr, personal interview)

the extended range, Ralph thought, *If the MiG pilot sees my tracers going between the two airplanes, he'll immediately forget Garrison and become defensive with me and firing my guns will also clear my previous gun jam.*

The left photo shows the gun sight with the aircraft flying straight and level with the pipper centered in the screen. The right photo shows the aircraft in a hard right turn. You can see where the guns are aiming (gun line); however, due to the G forces in the turn, the actual track of the bullets will stream low and left of the gun line, so the pilot must pull even more Gs in order for the pipper and the gun line to become superimposed for good hits.

Ralph gave him a short squirt of his .50-caliber guns, sending a sheet of tracers out, and then it was 'Katie, bar the door'. That guy was sharp. Ralph was sitting in the saddle and quickly found that he could perform any maneuver that the enemy could and just as well while maintaining his aircraft in firing position.[81] Ralph kept

---

[81] Ralph remembered, "I'm sure that we looked like two synchronized dancers up there flailing through the air while maintaining perfect position on one another."

his pipper (a small dot in the reticle of an optical or computing sight) about half a pipper width under the MiG. Ralph's wingman (#4) was sharp as a tack and he'd hacked a clock at the start of the fight. He told Ralph during the debrief that it took six minutes before Ralph got his first shot on that MiG. Each pilot jockeying for better position on his opponent, the incredibly intense six-minute dogfight had begun at 41,000 feet and bottomed out at 3,000 feet.

In the interim, other MiGs were all maneuvering, attempting to get Ralph off him. Ralph's maneuvering was so violent that he wasn't worried about them being able to slip in behind him.

If they could turn any tighter, then more power to 'em, he thought. Ralph was max performing his bird, pushing it to the limit the entire time. But he still couldn't get his pipper lined up on the enemy, so there was no sense in pulling the trigger. His extended range meant that his ammo would fall well short thus rendered ineffective.

Ralph's personal rule of thumb was anytime he pulled the trigger, he wanted the right sight picture, well within parameters, virtually guaranteeing good hits. He found that whenever he was patient, his bullets always found their target.

The nose art on Ralph's F-86 shows his name on the rail, red stars representing 10 MiG kills, the squadron insignia, and his first wife's name. Incidentally, two more red stars were added with a 'D' in the center of the star, representing two damaged aircraft.

Ralph's personal rule of thumb was anytime he pulled the trigger, he wanted the right sight picture, well within parameters, virtually guaranteeing good hits. He found that whenever he was patient, his bullets always found their target.

When the fighting cluster of MiGs and Sabres fought their way down to about 3,000 feet, the enemy MiGs rolled out on a northwesterly heading towards their safe haven on the opposite side of the Yalu River. Ralph rolled out too, each at max power and in a straight and level tail chase. Ralph allowed his pipper to settle down on the enemy for a little more than a second and at the outer edge of his gun range.[82] Ralph heard the dull but

---

[82] (R. S. Parr, personal interview)

rapid rumble and felt the tingling vibration in his feet and seat as he squeezed the trigger providing a one-second burst of gunfire, blowing the MiG's engine apart. The MiG was totally engulfed in fire and shredding parts and the immediate loss of thrust exponentially increased Ralph's closure rate.

As the MiG visually doubled in size in Ralph's windscreen due to the closure, he raked him up to the top of the fuselage with another hail of gunfire. Seeing his loss of thrust and smoke trail, Ralph immediately raced up behind him and skidded into a half roll to go over the top of his left wing while looking down into his cockpit. He saw the bloodied and disfigured pilot leaning forward, limp body hanging against his shoulder harness, and his head hovering over the stick. The now pilotless MiG silently descended like a glider toward earth with thick, black smoke billowing, while engine parts and blow torch-like flames spewed some 300 feet out its tail.

As Ralph scanned the MiG from above, he saw that the side of his airplane appeared ripped, like it had passed through a threshing machine. In a 'game of winner takes all', Ralph felt a slight sense of relief as the MiG soon went down in a ball of fire.[83]

His sense of relief was immediately replaced with a feeling of terror. As the one MiG impacted the ground, he simultaneously heard the banging of another MiG's .37 and .23-mm gunfire hammering away, sending a cascade of bullets and tracers in his direction. Ralph immediately started rolling his aircraft while looking over one shoulder, then swung his head around to look the other

---

[83] (R. S. Parr, personal interview)

direction and picked out the guy who was overshooting him. Ralph frantically pulled the stick as hard as he could, attempting to pull his aircraft around behind the MiG, gaining the edge as he slid into firing position. Ralph thought, *This pilot isn't nearly as talented as the first guy*, just before logging his second kill of the day before the MiG leaked out of range.

Ralph had this image painted on the back of his leather jacket depicting the MiG-15 kill.

Sucking hard on his oxygen hose, Ralph's mask was working overtime as he stole a quick five seconds to catch his breath while looking over each shoulder to clear behind his aircraft.[84] His wingman (#4) was also clearing

---

[84] Ralph remembered, "I had just been through more action than most of my buddies saw in five sorties. I needed a quick breather." A pilot clears behind his aircraft by turning his head to its right and left limit while combining turns in order

his tail, ensuring that no other adversaries were currently targeting Ralph.

Ralph's day was still far from over. As soon as he and his wingman ensured that their tails were clear, Ralph picked up two more MiGs that were low and in a perfect position for him to bounce. As Ralph rolled in on the bounce, he heard Garrison call over the radio, using the code word for the commander, Jimmy Johnson. Garrison said that Johnson was in trouble with a flamed-out engine and MiGs were all over him. He was requesting Ralph's immediate help.

Ralph said, "I'm on it!"

Ralph immediately broke off the engagement with the two aircraft he'd started to bounce and cranked his aircraft around in the general direction of Johnson's last known position, where he quickly picked him up visually. Ralph and his wingman came storming in to join the fight. There's an old rule stating: 'Never join a dogfight in progress.' This was one time when Ralph would break that rule. As they entered the fight, the MiGs thankfully broke away without firing a shot at Johnson and Ralph and his wingman escorted him out over the water. Johnson worked feverishly in the cockpit of his dead airplane, running multiple emergency procedure checklists until he finally got his engine cranked up at about 6,000 feet. Apparently, he flamed out his own engine as he flew up behind a MiG a bit too close. His shots blew the MiG apart, forcing him to swallow too many enemy aircraft parts through his intake.

---

to see if any adversaries are in or approaching firing position.

Ralph thought about his missed kill opportunities minutes before, but he'd just saved the commander's ass, so he wasn't disappointed. [85]

The four Sabres returned to base, recovered safely, and the debrief was extremely detailed as they went through each engagement, attempting to cipher exactly what happened and when. Garrison had a lot more to say to Ralph about 30 minutes after the debrief. He had received a rather one-sided phone call from the Fifth Air Force Commander.

The Fifth Air Force Commander had just gotten off the phone with the commander of Far Eastern Air Forces who said, "We're court-martialing Ralph Parr today because he flew while he was grounded!"

Jimmy Johnson immediately jumped in and poured oil on the troubled waters, ensuring it would never happen again. He said, "I'll lay my neck on the chopping block, and we'll get it straightened out in-house." The big 'powers that be' allowed it and said he'd better get it straightened out.[86]

Ralph had acquired strep throat a couple weeks prior to that mission. That's when the flight surgeon grounded him for 23 days. He went an entire week without flying and wasn't happy about it. It was the first time that he had gone an extended period without flying. So, when he felt better, he put himself back on the flying schedule and went to fly that sortie without knowing that he had been formally taken off flying status, or grounded, on flight

---

[85] (R. S. Parr, personal interview)

[86] (R. S. Parr, personal interview)

orders by the flight doc. The air force calls it DNIF (pronounced 'D'nif') or 'Duty Not Involving Flying'.

After the mission, a very disgruntled flight surgeon said, "By God, this will teach you."

Ralph looked at him and said, "Doc, you just don't understand. You don't know how hard it was for me to get over here and fight this battle. There is no way in the world I want to sit on the ground, so fix me up and let me go fly."

The Doc fixed him up alright. He transfused multiple units of penicillin every day and put beeswax on his back side.[87]

Importance of Training & Competition

Humans rely on training and thrive on competition in nearly all aspects of life. Athletics is probably the best example but flight training and even your child sitting in the classroom, memorizing the ins and outs of the multiplication tables are prime examples. An athlete trains to achieve goals, like winning the state championship or an Olympic gold medal. The fighter pilot constantly trains to stay alive during a wicked air-to-air engagement while attempting to eliminate the enemy, and your child memorizes the multiplication tables to outperform their schoolmates in a classroom competition. Ralph's experiences were no different. His extensive training catapulted him to becoming one of the best gunnery pilots in the world. In 1953, he earned first place honors in the Far East gunnery tournament after the

---

[87] Ralph remembered, "I was one hurting guy and wasn't back to feeling 100% for quite some time."

Korean War. Earlier, in 1950, he was runner-up in the world-wide gunnery tournament.

John Roberts, one of Ralph's best friends, flew on the same gunnery team, earned first place honors in the worldwide, and second place in the Far East competition. Ralph and Roberts simply swapped the top two places for two years. Unfortunately, the 1951 and 1952 tournaments were scrubbed due to the Korean War.

A funny thing happened during one of the competition sorties.[88] The rules of engagement on these missions were:

1) Once you start your engine, you are accounted for every round of ammunition you have on board; and

2) If you lose radio communications, you must abort or cancel the mission, forcing you out of the competition.

John discovered a transmitter problem in his UHF radio during the preflight. Of course, he couldn't tell anybody about his maintenance issue because he couldn't transmit any communications. He didn't want to abort either. Ralph was the only pilot in the flight of four aircraft to realize that Roberts couldn't transmit. Ralph had to act quickly. He devised a plan in an attempt to keep John in the competition. Ralph knew that he could somewhat mimic John's voice, so he changed the pitch and inflection in his voice a bit when he talked on the radio. He began making all required radio calls for John during the entire sortie. In essence, Ralph had to make all the calls for both aircraft, using their assigned (different) call signs while in the air-to-air gunnery pattern. Ralph

---

[88] Ralph couldn't recall if this occurred in the 1950 or 1953 competition.

had to call high key, call in and call off the target for both of them, and he had to make damn sure that he had it right or risk disqualification.

The squadron commander, Colonel Garrison, was the flight lead on this sortie. Everything appeared to go smoothly but Ralph would have to wait to see if his change in voice inflection was a pass or a failure. After all aircraft had landed, Ralph called the flight and told them to switch their radio to their squadron common frequency, a discrete frequency monitored only by other squadron members. Garrison and the rest of the flight made the frequency change and checked in.

Garrison said, "Lead's up on frequency."

Ralph said: "This is two; just a heads up, four is currently without a radio."

Gene Serowik was flying as three and immediately piped up on the radio saying, "I don't think so. I've been listening to his radio calls the entire sortie."

Ralph grinned inside his oxygen mask and said, "You've been listening to me and I've been busier than a cat digging a hole in a marble floor!"

The gunnery pattern was a 360-degree track and Ralph had to keep situational awareness of where Roberts was in the pattern, make his radio calls, where Ralph was in the pattern, so he could make all his own transmissions while ensuring that all calls were made at the right time and place. Ralph's first attempt at ventriloquism had passed the test as their four-ship won that mission competition with an 80-percent success rate.

John Roberts retired as a four-star general as the commander of Air Training Command.[89] John had a habit of embarrassing Ralph when they'd see each other at the officer's club; John would stand at the top of the steps of the Auger Inn, and to entice Ralph, he'd say to a group of pilots, "See that guy there? There goes the greatest gunner in the United States Air Force."

A humbled Ralph would reply, "John, don't do that," shaking his head. He had a helluva sense of humor and they each enjoyed a good laugh out of every encounter.

Ralph's air-to-air gunnery skills were heavily tested the day he ran across a cluster of MiG formations, numbering up to 100 aircraft.[90] Thankful for the skills he'd developed through intense training and discipline, he picked one MiG-15 out of the bunch, quickly maneuvered his aircraft until the pipper was superimposed over the MiG, and then unleashed a three-second burst of gunfire.

Ralph earned immediate feedback on the success of his shots as his aircraft was sprayed with the enemy's shards of sheet metal as the aft portion of the MiG disintegrated in flight from 1,000 feet ahead. The still flyable MiG began a rapid descent for the cloud deck; Ralph lowered his nose to maintain firing position on him. Ralph had increased his closure rate during the

---

[89] Now Air Education and Training Command (AETC)

[90] Ralph remembered, "When I came across that beehive of MiGs, I momentarily made a cross with my two index fingers in the windscreen and counted 25 airplanes in the upper left quadrant. I multiplied that by four to realize the numbers we were up against."

descent and was right on the MiG's tail when he disappeared into the cloud. Now, in a severe whiteout with zero visibility, Ralph knew that he was still on him, so he squeezed the trigger one more time and saw an immediate bright, lightning-like flash illuminate within the cloud. A huge, unidentifiable piece of MiG went over the top of Ralph's left wing. As he exited the cloud, Ralph glanced over his right shoulder to see Al Dixon, his wingman, nestled tight on Ralph's right wing, witnessing all the action.

They immediately turned south and headed for home as they were running low on gas and knew that they were vastly outnumbered. When they arrived back home, they hopped out of their jets to perform the post-flight walk around and were walking across the baking tarmac back to the squadron. Ralph sensed that someone was looking over his shoulder, so he turned around and caught Dixon, who was on his tail by a few feet, staring with a semi-dazed look in his eyes.

Ralph said, "What's the matter, Al?"

Dixon released a heavy sigh, "I'm glad we don't do that every day!"

Ralph chuckled and said, "C'est la vie."

Al retired as a four-star general and has since passed away. Some people thought that he was nasty, crude, and a mean son-of-a-bitch, but Ralph found him to be very fair. He had a lot of intestinal fortitude, and he was careful to keep from hurting you. They shared a strong rapport between them.[91]

---

[91] (R. S. Parr, personal interview)

Chapter 10
When Last Was First

Ralph's eyes lit up. He snapped his head to the ten o'clock position and looked low. Was he seeing things? He leaned forward until his movement was abruptly blocked when his shoulder harness hit the stops. *What the hell is that?* he thought. Better yet, *WHO the hell is that?* He momentarily glanced towards the ground about two-thirds of the way out to the horizon to refocus his eyes for that distance, then looked again at the non-fighter type aircraft crossing the Yalu River and heading his direction. He knew that there were no 'heavies' scheduled to fly today. Who could it be then? The minutely detailed actions occurring in Ralph's cockpit over the next few minutes would spawn dramatic images, shocking thoughts, and implications lasting years.

Can you think of any instance in your life when the last was actually the first? The last United States aerial victory of the Korean War occurred on 27 July 1953, the final day of hostilities. It was Ralph's 10th kill of the war, earning him double ace distinction, but the first of its kind.

The shoot down of a Soviet IL-12 transport by a United States fighter aircraft in the Korean theatre on July 27 was reported in the August 1, 1953 issue of the

New York Times. The Soviets described the attack on their transport aircraft as 'pirate like', and they reserved the right to demand compensation for those who died. The question begging the answer is whether a 'tit-for-tat' was involved in the shootdown of a United States RB-50 aircraft two days later, on 29 July. A Soviet protest over the shootdown of the Soviet transport by Korean-based United States Air Force fighters presented the Soviet Union's views on their loss:

IL-12

On July 27, 1953 at 06:28 Moscow time, four American fighters, after crossing the border of the Democratic Republic of China, attacked and shot down a Russian IL-12 transport aircraft that was flying from Port Arthur to Vladivostok. This occurred near the city of Khnadyan, 110 kilometers from the Sino-Soviet border. The aircraft burned up, and the six crew members and 15 passengers on board were killed.

The Soviets also informed the government of the Democratic Republic of Korea and the Chinese government that the Soviet Union had sent the two latest demarches, and recommended that the Chinese government protest to the Americans this violation of the Korean/Chinese border, tying in other Korean border violations by American aircraft. A number of heated diplomatic exchanges ensued without reaching any mutual agreements between the aggrieved parties.[92]

Information concerning Ralph's IL-12 shoot down was declassified 50 years after the war had ended, but the intricate details of the events going on inside his cockpit during the first half of the sortie were a circus of events. Preflight, taxi and takeoff roll were uneventful, but then things went a little crazy. As he broke ground, Ralph watched the airspeed increase, noted two positive climbs (as he glanced across the altimeter and vertical velocity indicator) just as he'd done thousands of times before.

Next, he reached down to raise the gear handle up in compliance with his after takeoff/climb checklist. The gear handle wouldn't budge. His gear wouldn't come up. Dumbfounded, he fiddled around with the gear handle as it now drew all of his attention and he thought that he may have to abort his final mission of the war. Or at least turn back toward the base, land, and taxi back in to get another jet. Continuing to 'fly the aircraft' as he'd been taught during every phase of pilot training, he thought that he'd try it one more time to see if he could get the gear up and continue with the scheduled sortie. Ralph grabbed the gear handle in one last futile attempt to

---

[92] (Tart and Keefe)

actuate it, and this time he heard and felt an abnormal 'clunk'. The gear finally came up, but it resulted in an even bigger problem. The entire gear handle came off in his hand. He thought, *Shit, this is a first for me!* He decided to leave the gear in place, in the up and locked position, temporarily store the gear handle on the glare shield and work the issue during the recovery phase back to base.

**JET ACE GETS FINAL KILL OF WAR—AN IL-12.
The 36th jet ace of the war, Capt. Ralph Parr of Apple
Valley, California, is shown in this picture, reading
about the truce signing. His final kill—an ironic 'first',
in that he shot down the first IL-12 of the Korean War—
turned out to be, in addition, the final aircraft loss
inflicted on the enemy before cease-fire.**

He didn't want to sit out this mission with the armistice 12 hours from going into effect.

The mission was fragged to escort a marine photo reconnaissance aircraft up to the northern-most airfields to prove that at the cease fire time, on the last day of the war, there were no enemy aircraft on the field. No one had ever gone that far north; at least Ralph hadn't. A larger aircraft, type unknown appeared in his windscreen, abeam and coming toward him. Ralph picked him up visually before the aircraft exited China into Korean airspace. Ralph was flying near Chunggang-jin on the

Yalu River. Fifth Air Force had instructed pilots to keep the pressure on them that last day until the appointed time.

Ralph called him out to the flight and the escort leader said, "Keep your eye on him." He pressed on and the Yalu River made some easily identifiable turns along the border.

Ralph positively identified where he was before he started the engagement. He was well aware of the fact that he didn't want to make a careless or stupid mistake on the last day of the war, which could jeopardize the impending armistice. After the twin-engine prop crossed the Chinese border and was well within North Korea, Ralph called the mission leader back and asked for permission to go down and visually check him out. From a distance, the aircraft looked like a United States aircraft on a psychological warfare mission used for broadcasting propaganda to the enemy. Ralph checked him out once, rolled back up, thought about it for a moment, then went back down and checked him out again. He knew that he wasn't imagining things. It was a Soviet IL-12, a twin-engine aircraft visually similar to the United States' Curtiss Commando C-46. That's why he wanted to take a couple of looks at it to positively identify it because he didn't want to make any mistakes regarding the target and his location during the engagement.[93]

The aircraft was adorned with red-star markings and portrayed no civilian markings. Ralph pulled up and over the top and made a right to left high-side pass. Then when he hit his 'in range' designation, he thought that

---

[93] (R. S. Parr, personal interview)

he'd start on the left engine to see if he could at least force him down. His own gun camera film showed the intense hits on the left engine. Ralph made one gun pass behind and off to the right side of his aircraft. As he turned to come back around for another pass, he saw that the aircraft was totally engulfed in flames and then exploded in midair, becoming his 10th kill of the war.[94] He had no idea that the engagement would be so highly scrutinized by the Soviets and draw lengthy interrogations by U.S. Government attorneys.

Ralph was able to reinstall the gear handle during his return to the base, not permanently but just enough to actuate the gear mechanism, enabling him to land safely.

A SECRET Intelligence report, declassified in recent years, highlighted the last kill of the war as being a 'first'. The information was provided by the Air Force Historical Research Agency and was listed under section of the report labeled: Enemy Air Activity. It read:

"Even on the last day of the Korean conflict, a new historical 'first' was recorded as a result of aerial activity over Korea. Some two hours and twenty-five minutes after the signing of the armistice agreement and prior to the ceasefire, the first IL-12 was shot down over North Korea by a Sabre jet. Two Sabre pilots on combat patrol in the Yalu River Area observed an enemy IL-12 (with red stars on the wings, tail, and fuselage) flying east, 35 miles northeast of Kanggye, at 6,000 feet. The friendly leader made two identifying passes and then made a firing pass, observing hits over the entire enemy

---

[94] (R. S. Parr, personal interview)

aircraft. Both engines began to burn, prior to the aircraft exploding. An IL-12 is one of the twin-engine transport-type aircraft assigned to the Communist Air Forces in China."

LAST PLANE DOWNED WAS "FIRST"

On the last day of the war, Capt. Ralph S. Parr, a jet ace from Apple Valley, California, was on the last fighter-sweep near the Yalu before the cease-fire went into effect—looking for enemy planes. He found one and shot down the last plane of the war, ironically an IL-12, first to be shot down in Korea. Map below shows where the IL-12 went down. Pictures above and below, left, show IL-12 that landed at Haneda AFB, Japan, 23 September 52 from Vladivostok.

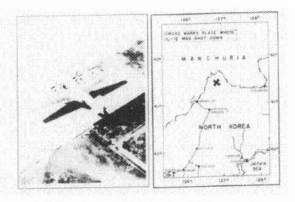

The kill drew extreme scrutiny over the next five days. Ralph endured 56 hours of interrogation from State Department lawyers. The Soviet Union sued the USAF and Ralph personally, accusing him of penetrating Chinese airspace by more than 200 miles in order to shoot the IL-12 down. Those allegations were completely false. He knew precisely where he was because he had double-checked the bends in the river where the IL-12 went in.[95] After the lengthy interrogations and the passage of time, the Soviet Union dropped all charges one week prior to the statute of limitations. Four separate official reports read:

"On 27 July 1953, an Aeroflot IL-12 *Coach* was shot down by US Air Force F-86F Sabre pilot Ralph Parr, near Kanggye, North Korea, shortly before the armistice went into effect. All 21 people on board were killed. The Soviets claimed that the aircraft was actually over the People's Republic of China when shot down."

---

[95] (R. S. Parr, personal interview)

"'On 27 July 1953, CPT Ralph Parr spotted an IL-12 transport from the 83rd IAK that was transferring pilots. He shot it down with full loss of life (23 KIA).' The Soviets were furious. It was clearly marked as a Soviet (e.g. Red Stars) and they sued (Ralph) in the World Court for wrongful deaths and liability for loss. It took several years but the court finally ruled that the aircraft was in what could be considered a war zone and ergo took its chances."

"27-July-53, IL-12 Capt. Dmitry Glinany 593 OTAP (Soviet) shot down by F-86 USAF (20 on board killed)."

"July 27, 1953: A negotiated ceasefire ends the 'shooting war' in Korea. The same day, U.S. Air Force Capt. Ralph S. Parr, flying an F-86 Sabre, shoots down a Soviet Ilyushin IL-12 transport, reportedly 'the last kill' of the Korean War."

Ralph made ace in 11 days and from the time he got his first enemy kill to the time he got his tenth, and last, spanning 30 missions in five weeks.

A typical Korean War combat mission began with an incredibly detailed briefing. The overall mission timing was driven by your takeoff time or the time your flight began its takeoff roll. Ralph covered everything imaginable in his pre-briefs, including contingencies in order to negate any unforeseen circumstances. After the mission, a debrief of the same detail and magnitude followed. A pilot, especially the young and inexperienced, learns more from the debrief than a pre-brief.[96]

---

[96] (R. S. Parr, personal interview)

The pre-brief merely details for the pilots in your flight, the plan for that particular mission that particular day. The pre-brief emphasizes tactics and strategies that you'll employ throughout the sortie. On the other hand, the debriefing allows you to discuss mission information stored from all members of the flight, including the small things that may have gone unnoticed or that really didn't go as planned. After thorough discussion, you learn, adapt, and implement any changes required for your next sortie to enhance safety, ensuring mission success. Ralph always strived for perfection but counted on constant improvement on every mission he flew.[97]

Most of the engagements began at around 40,000 feet. The MiGs flew as high as they could fly, sometimes even above their published max ceiling.

The Americans knew that the majority of MiG drivers were not Korean or Chinese pilots. They didn't speak Chinese over the radios. They spoke a different language.

The opening of archives in the former Soviet Union confirmed a fact that had long been denied—the USSR provided many of the MiG-15 pilots and units that fought in MiG Alley. Like their U.S. Air Force opponents, several of these Soviet pilots were World War II combat veterans.

Before the Korean War, Soviet pilots were already in China, training the newly-created communist Chinese Air Force, or People's Liberation Army Air Force (PLAAF). In August 1950, the USSR secretly deployed MiG-15s to Antung next to the border with North Korea. Soviet

---

[97] (R. S. Parr, personal interview)

MiG-15 pilots flew their first combat missions over North Korea in early November 1950.

The Soviets tried to hide their nationality and denied that they had pilots in direct combat. Their MiG-15s had North Korean or Chinese markings. Soviet pilots received orders to only speak Korean phrases over the radio (although F-86 pilots heard them speaking Russian over the radio in the heat of combat). Despite these precautions, USAF pilots reported seeing non-Asian pilots flying the MiGs. Sabre pilots also noticed the difference in experience when less-skilled North Korean and Chinese pilots also began flying MiG-15s against them—they nicknamed the more-capable Soviet pilots 'Honchos' (Japanese for 'boss'). The fact that Soviet pilots were flying the MiGs became an open secret.[98]

A few months after the war ended, an article in 'Colliers' magazine by Gen. Mark Clark was published regarding the Russians having two air armies with an accompaniment of more than 400 fighter pilots to gain combat experience. Ralph heard people say over the years that they were lousy shots or they couldn't fly very well. In reality, they were just like American pilots. Some of them were so damned sharp that it would scare you to death in nearly all flight regimes.[99]

The Yalu River divides North Korea and Manchuria and was a boundary not to be crossed by United Nations forces. Once you got your aircraft and your opponent's aircraft in the telephone booth size of airspace during an intense dogfight, pursuit and the need to keep your ass

---

[98] (Soviet Pilots over MiG Alley)

[99] (R. S. Parr, personal interview)

alive took over. Once engaged in the fight, you didn't have a large map spread over your thighs, tracking all your visual ground references. You concentrated on keeping your eyes on the opponent who was attempting to kill you. In fact, in a dogfight, you frequently didn't even know which side was up as you countered every move he made. It was like a game of chess, keeping as many moves in front of you and hoping, in the end, you had more conquering moves remaining than he had.[100]

It was eerie up north because from 30 miles on south side of the Yalu River, you could see enemy airfields with airplanes taking off and landing. It was awfully frustrating for Ralph knowing that he could only go so far north when he could see the enemy aircraft in flight but still in their 'safe area'. Ralph had no doubt there were Chinese pilots flying. There were North Korean pilots flying and he knew damned well that there were Russians flying. He ran across two or three superior pilots during his time who were frighteningly skilled, leaving no doubt that they were experts.[101]

In the end, the Americans downed 14 enemy MiGs for every F-86 lost in combat.[102]

Once the armistice took effect, the Korean peninsula was divided into two nations with each country, keeping

---

[100] (R. S. Parr, personal interview)

[101] Ralph remembered, "I know I faced a few 'Honchos' from time to time. There was no comparison; they were the best pilots the enemy had to offer."

[102] 14:1 MiG to F-86 kill ratio were the figures Ralph recalled, although you may find slightly different numbers available from various sources.

a watchful eye on the other and maintaining heavily fortified forces on each side of the border. Even after the end of hostilities, there was no love lost between the two sides. This would soon be proven with the advent of 'Operation *Moolah*'.

During the Korean War, the Russian-built Mikoyan-Gurevich-15 swept-wing jet fighter proved to be a superior plane as it first engaged pilots of the United Nations. With a range of 745 miles, the MiG-15 was a match for, if not better than, the few American jets available, even the F-86 Sabre jet. The MiG-15 was a high-altitude interceptor that was well armed and could remain in the air for over an hour.

Because of its superiority, the Soviet Union went to extreme measures to prevent one of the planes from falling into UN hands. Simultaneously, the UN was making every effort to get hold of a MiG for study. Russian pilots, flying with North Korea, were under orders not to fly over South Korean territory and, if possible, to avoid sorties over the water for fear that they might crash and the UN would be able to salvage the wreckage. Those flying the MiG-15 for the Chinese were required to have Chinese Air Force markings on their planes, wear Chinese uniforms, and speak only Chinese on the radio.

As all other options seemed to have failed, the United States Air Force decided to try to obtain one of the Soviet planes with a bribe and thus unleashed the highly controversial effort identified as Operation *Moolah*.

In this plan, the joint chiefs of staff offered $50,000 and political asylum to any pilot who would deliver a fully operational MiG to a UN-occupied air base. The agreement also promised an extra $50,000 for the first plane to be delivered.

There had been several earlier attempts to capture a downed MiG. Despite the fact that a few had been spotted, the military had been unable to get the kind of data they wanted. In April 1951, when the United Nations became aware of a downed MiG-15 no more than 100 miles inland, an operation was launched to find the plane that had crashed. The plane was nearly intact and located on a sandbar. The Chinese committed several unsuccessful bombing runs, attempting to destroy it. When retrieval efforts failed due to constant harassment by the enemy, Captain David Nichols of the United States Air Force, assigned to the Office of Special Investigation, flew to the spot with a crew of five specialists. There he managed to photograph the plane in considerable detail. During the flight back, enemy forces attacked their helicopter. The chopper was heavily damaged but managed to get back safely. Nichols received a distinguished service citation for his courageous action.

Several persons vied to take credit for the idea behind Operation *Moolah*. The *Saturday Evening Post* reported that the idea had come from the Russian Research Center at Harvard University, but the university denied having suggested it. The think-tank headed by Alan K. Abner, then a captain in the Psychological Warfare Branch, took some credit for it; General Mark Clark remembered that the idea had been first suggested by a newspaper man named Edward Hymoff of the International News Service and that he had been well into his drink at the time. Regardless of who was responsible for the idea, it was picked up by someone and taken on to Washington and approved.

But how best to let the enemy know of the offer? The military assumed that most of the planes would be flown by Russian pilots, so the first broadcast of the offer was made in Russian and sent out through the First Radio Broadcasting Leaflet Group. It was also released in a series of second broadcasts, in Korean and Chinese, on UN radio, 'the Voice of the United Nations Command'. The Russian language broadcasts created something of a problem, because while there was no doubt that Soviet pilots were operating in Korea, every effort had been made by both sides to avoid acknowledging it. On April 22, 1952, when Colonel Yevgeni Pepelyayeu was awarded the Golden Star of the heroes of the Soviet Union, he wore civilian clothes and there was no mention of where he had been fighting.

To further extend the word of the offer, more than half a million leaflets were dropped over MiG airfields in Sinuiju and Uiji. On the front of the leaflet was a letter from General Mark Clark that promised: "The Far East Command will reward 50,000 United States dollars to any pilot who delivers a modern, operational, combat-type jet aircraft of flyable condition to South Korea. The first pilot who delivers such a jet aircraft to the free world will receive an additional bonus of 50,000 U.S. dollars for his bravery."

On the back of the leaflets was some variation of this message: "Courageous pilot! If you like freedom . . . If you have courage . . . If you want to live a better, honorable life . . . This is your opportunity of once in a thousand years. Free yourself from communist tyranny. Fly your jet toward the free world."

No communist pilots responded to this astounding offer during the course of the war. It was not until September 21, 1953, nearly two months after the signing of the ceasefire, that a North Korean pilot, Lieutenant No Kum-Sok, landed his MiG-15 fighter at Kimpo Air Field.

MiG-15 in the Korean War Gallery at the National Museum of the United States Air Force.

Landing downwind, he taxied to the alert shack and parked his plane next to an F-86 in which pilot, John Lowery, was sitting. At first, the astonished airmen at the field, totally unaware of the offer, did not know what to do. Eventually, Tom Feltman, an Alabama airman who was at the base, arrived in a Jeep and accepted the Korean officer's surrender.

Kum-Sok, it turned out, was not aware of the award being offered. Rather, he claimed that he had been raised by Catholic missionaries and that he'd always wanted to come to the United States. He had defected at the first opportunity because he had grown disillusioned with communism and wanted to live in America. Deserting was his only chance to do so.

By the time the North Korean pilot set down his MiG-15, most in the military had totally forgotten that the award had been offered. Dwight D. Eisenhower, the newly elected president, acknowledged that he had never heard of such an offer and thought that it was unethical. Besides, he believed that if a man wanted to defect, it should be for political reasons, not for money. He also argued that if the offer had been made, it was now made invalid by the ceasefire. Interestingly, there was considerable disapproval from the allies and the press. One labor peer told the House of Commons that it was a 'dastardly thing'. Winston Churchill agreed that it was a legitimate act of war but stressed that the timing was bad.

Life for the Korean defector was mixed. He did not get all the money that had been promised, but he did become an American citizen. In due time, the North Korean pilot changed his name to Kenneth Rowe and was eventually granted American citizenship. He was publicly given a check to satisfy some public expectations, but he gave most of it back. He secured government help in finishing his education, and after a time, he was able to complete a Bachelor of Science degree from the University of Delaware and went to complete a Master's in engineering. He worked with Chuck Yeager and Tom Collins in the operation and flight-testing of the defected MiG-15 and later worked for the University of North Dakota, DuPont, Boeing,

General Dynamics, Lockheed Martin, General Motors, and Northrop-Grumman. After that, he had several teaching positions in aeronautical engineering. Despite all the fuss that had been made about capturing a MiG, neither the military nor the public reacted strongly once it had been accomplished.

So, how did the communists react to the event? Following the defection, the Soviet Air Force called a stand-down for eight days, during which no MiGs were allowed to leave the ground. No explanation was ever given for this unusual action but some suggested that it was to give the government time to do another quick check on the loyalty of its pilots. It was later reported that the communists also took several reprisals that included the death of Lieutenant Kon So-Sung. Lieutenant Kon had apparently been aware of Lieutenant No's plans but had not turned him in and paid the ultimate price.[103]

Ralph was at Kimpo Airfield (K-14) in Seoul, South Korea, when the armistice was signed, ending hostilities in the Korean War. It was a very exciting time. They got all of the Korean War Aces from the 4th Fighter Wing together for a photo. That photo sat atop Ralph's dresser until the day he passed. It was a great group of guys who were at the height of their careers, jubilant and happy that the armistice signaled an end to the conflict.

---

[103] (Edwards)

"Five Men; Fifty-Five MiGs"
Pictured from left are Lonny Moore, Vermont Garrison,
James K. Johnson, Ralph S. Parr, and Jimmy Jabara.
The photo was staged near the flight line at Kimpo, in
celebration of the armistice signing.

Signing Armistice Agreement for the Restoration of the South Korean State (1953)

While Ralph and his fellow pilots were engaging MiGs in horrific dogfights on a daily basis, things back home were not so good. The Korean War was the first war that the United States population didn't thoroughly back. It was a war where the military, for the first time, had large amounts of input from outside military channels on how it should be fought. Because it was not a popular war, people still knew what was going on due to newspaper accounts, yet it seemed that nobody really cared. There was no rationing or cutting back during that time like in WWII; therefore, it didn't receive much attention and people just weren't interested in supporting a war effort that didn't directly affect them at home.[104]

The Korean War, which began on June 25, 1950, when the North Koreans invaded South Korea, officially

---

[104] (R. S. Parr, personal interview)

ended on July 27, 1953. At 10 a.m., in Panmunjom, scarcely acknowledging each other, U.S. Army Lt. Gen. William K. Harrison, Jr., senior delegate, United Nations Command Delegation; North Korean Gen. Nam Il, senior delegate, Delegation of the Korean People's Army and the Chinese people's volunteers, signed 18 official copies of the tri-language Korean Armistice Agreement.

It was the end of the longest negotiated armistice in history: 158 meetings spread over two years and 17 days. That evening at 10:00 p.m., the truce went into effect. The Korean Armistice Agreement is somewhat exceptional in that it is purely a military document—no nation is a signatory to the agreement. Specifically, the armistice agreement:

- Suspended open hostilities.
- Withdrew all military forces and equipment from a 4,000-meter-wide zone, establishing the 'Demilitarized Zone' as a buffer between the forces.
- Prevented both sides from entering the air, ground, or sea areas under control of the other.
- Arranged release and repatriation of prisoners of war and displaced persons.
- Established the Military Armistice Commission (MAC) and other agencies to discuss any violations and to ensure adherence to the truce terms.
- The armistice, while it stopped hostilities, was not a permanent peace treaty between nations.

President Eisenhower, who was keenly aware of the 1.8 million American men and women who had served in Korea and the 36,576 Americans who had died there, played a key role in bringing about a cease-fire. In announcing the agreement to the American people in a television address shortly after the signing, he said, in part:

Soldiers, sailors, and airmen of 16 different countries have stood as partners beside us throughout these long and bitter months. In this struggle, we have seen the United Nations meet the challenge of aggression—not with pathetic words of protest but with deeds of decisive purpose. And so, at long last, the carnage of war is to cease and the negotiation of the conference table is to begin. . . . [We hope that] all nations may come to see the wisdom of composing differences in this fashion before, rather than after, there is resort to brutal and futile battle.

Now as we strive to bring about that wisdom, there is, in this moment of sober satisfaction, one thought that must discipline our emotions and steady our resolution. It is this: We have won an armistice on a single battleground—not peace in the world. We may not now relax our guard nor cease our quest.

President Eisenhower concluded his announcement by quoting from Abraham Lincoln's second inaugural address.[105]

Ralph's Korean War flying days were through but his legacy and historic flying record will be read and digested forever. In June 1953, Ralph downed eight MiG-

---

[105] (Armistice Agreement for the Restoration of the South Korean State (1953))

15s and one more in July. Then he shot down the IL-12 transport on July 27, his last, and the final kill of the Korean War. The armistice was signed at 1001L on July 27 and took effect 12 hours later.

Ralph Parr's Record of Korean War MiG Kills

Date	Aircraft
7 June 53	2 MiGs
10 June 53	1 MiG
18 June 53	2 MiGs
19 June 53	1 MiG
30 June 53	2 MiGs
12 July 53	1 MiG
27 July 53	1 IL-12

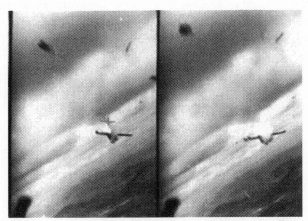

4th MiG-15 Kill 18 June 1953

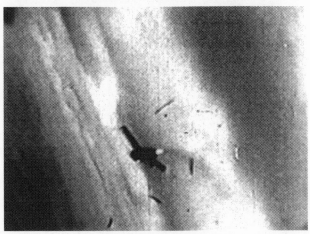

5th MiG-15 Kill 18 June 1953

**A poster was designed and rightly named 'MiG Maulers
of the Korean War, 1950-1953', depicting photos of the
USAF Korean War Aces on playing cards.**

USAF Korean War Aces

First Name	Last Name	Total Credits
JOSEPH	MCCONNELL JR	16
JAMES	JABARA	15
MANUEL	FERNANDEZ JR	14.5
GEORGE	DAVIS JR	13
FREDERICK	BLESSE	10
HAROLD	FISCHER	10
JAMES	JOHNSON	10
LONNIE	MOORE	10
RALPH	PARR JR	10
CECIL	FOSTER	9
JAMES	LOW	9
JAMES	HAGERSTROM	8.5
ROBINSON	RISNER	8
GEORGE	RUDDELL	8
CLIFFORD	JOLLEY	7
LEONARD	LILLEY	7
HENRY	BUTTELMANN	7
GEORGE	JONES	6.5
FRANCIS	GABRESKI	6.5
DONALD	ADAMS	6.5
WINTON	MARSHAL	6.5
JAMES	KASLER	6
ROBERT	LOVE	6
WILLIAM	WHISNER JR	5.5
DOLPHIN	OVERTON III	5
WILLIAM	WESCOTT	5
CLYDE	CURTIN	5

STEPHEN	BETTINGER	5
IVEN	KINCHELOE JR	5
RICHARD	BECKER	5
ROBERT	MOORE	5
ROBERT	LATSHAW JR	5
ROBERT	BALDWIN	5
RICHARD	CREIGHTON	5
RALPH	GIBSON	5
HARRISON	THYNG	5

Chapter 11
Vietnam

The late 1960's was a tumultuous time around the world, with life-changing events arming the three national network anchors with an abundance of news to convey to their nightly viewers. Earning numerous air time minutes were stories of astronauts Gus Grissom, Edward White, and Roger Chaffee perishing in an Apollo 1 capsule fire during a simulated launch back in January and the end of the Arab-Israeli 6-Day War was only three months removed. United States troop levels in Vietnam were approaching 500,000, exceeding the Korean War figures at its peak, sparking riotous domestic antiwar protests that would climax during a march on the Pentagon in October.

It was September 1967, a time when everyone serving in the air force was destined to serve two tours in Vietnam. Ralph was in that mix with his tours spanning from September 1967 to September 1968, as group commander of the 12th Tactical Fighter Wing (TFW) at Cam Ranh Bay, and then as commander of the 12th TFW at Phu Cat[106] from March 1970 to February 1971.

---

[106] Cam Ranh Bay and Phu Cat are two air bases located on the east coast of South Vietnam. The 12th TFW moved from

Ralph arrived for his first Vietnam tour at Cam Ranh Bay as a full bird colonel, which always turns heads in the squadron. At the time, he had no idea that the Green Bay Packers would beat the Oakland Raiders in Super Bowl II[107] in three months, but did realize that now, in a place he called home, in a country comparable to the size of New Mexico, the squadron pilots were attempting to gain a 'good read' on him as quickly as possible. They wanted to see if he was going to be a good fit in the group, or whether he was coming back for one last cockpit tour before retirement as a 'desk jockey',[108] and fly like one too.

The fighter pilots who'd flown 20-plus missions were often convinced that they knew it all and thought here comes this new kid on the block with all his rank; he's probably not going to do anything but fly a desk. They're thinking, he's brand new to the game and doesn't fully understand what's going on here. Would the new boss be 'that colonel' who adds his name to the flight schedule for the simple, once a month square filler sortie? Ralph knew that they initially wouldn't want to listen to new thoughts or ideas. He also knew that their thought process and overall acceptance of him would increase as he gained experience, learned the local procedures and

---

Cam Ranh Bay to Phu Cat on 1 April 1970, allowing Ralph to serve in the same wing twice but at two separate bases.

[107] Packers beat the Raiders 33-14 in Super Bowl II in Miami's Orange Bowl on 14 January 1968.

[108] A person who's job is to work behind a desk and in this case, not fly airplanes (often).

established good working relationships, forging earned trust. It doesn't hurt to be 'a good stick' too.

Ralph had three fighter combat tours under his belt by that time and a complete understanding of air-to-air and air-to-ground operations, and most importantly, what it takes to perform each safely. He needed to exude his wisdom by being a good mentor but not preach or boast of his past success to avoid any negative labeling or hasty judgments by his troops.[109]

He now was in command of four F-4 squadrons at Cam Ranh Bay, all of which were employing non-standard in-flight procedures. For example, the flight schedulers could place one pilot from each of the four squadrons in a flight of four aircraft, and at some point during the mission, it would get downright dangerous out there because they were all flying non-standard procedures. Not one was 'on the same sheet of music'. In fact, they were flying as four individuals rather than four individuals flying as a team of one.

Cam Ranh Bay was suffering a fair amount of combat losses and Ralph was hand-picked to command the group and aggressively address this problem. After he'd been in country about a month, he presented a new set of rules based on his previous experience, attempting to reverse the aircraft loss rate. He thought that it was ill-advised to continue relearning from old mistakes and implementing fixes haphazardly using varying techniques totally dependent on which squadron you belonged.

Ralph implemented sound procedures across the board, forcing all pilots to abide by the same set of group

---

[109] (R. S. Parr, personal interview)

standards and procedures so that any pilot could fly with another from any squadron on any given day and all in flight changes would appear transparent through standardization. Everyone would now know what to expect because they all procedurally flew the same way and implemented similar tactics during combat. The immediate results were amazing. Smoother and safer flying operations were welcomed changes at that point of the Vietnam War.

The aircraft loss rates plummeted from somewhere around 2.3 aircraft losses per month to one aircraft downed over the next 10 months. Ralph's message hit home.[110]

As the group director of operations (DO), Ralph flew with whomever he chose. He flew operational missions in conjunction with his duties as the group commander. One day, the 7 AF Commander called him and said, "My staff insists that as a leader, you're flying too much, Ralph. You're flying too many operational combat missions in the group commander position and it just doesn't look good."

Ralph vehemently replied, "If you care to check the aircraft loss rate of this outfit, it's in bad shape, so somebody's got to show them how to do it right. What is a better way than to personally show them?"[111]

Ralph's four squadrons lost but one aircraft over the next ten months. In that particular mishap, the back seater was killed, and the pilot barely got out but survived the crash.

---

[110] (R. S. Parr, personal interview)

[111] (R. S. Parr, personal interview)

The pilot was rushed back to base for his medical examination on a Scatback, a small aircraft used in those days to deliver pilots to out-bases. He stepped from the Scatback and headed straight for base ops.[112] He hopped in a staff car that was parked out front and headed directly to Ralph's office.

He burst into Ralph's office and while still trying to catch his breath, said, "Sir, I crashed one of your airplanes today, killing my backseater. I want you to be the first to know that I did it doing precisely what you said don't ever do. I just knew I could complete the maneuver this time, but my failure cost me."

Ralph could see the heartfelt anguish in the young pilot's eyes. After a pregnant pause and some thought, Ralph said, "Do you want to make up for your buddy's loss? Go tell others your story, teaching them to implement exactly what I taught you so that a tragic loss of this nature never happens again." The pilot, never losing eye contact, slowly nodded and departed Ralph's office in military fashion.

Apparently, the pilot and his WSO were attacking an anti-aircraft gun one-on-one. Ralph always taught his young pilots, "You must remember that it's not the gun emplacement you're targeting that will kill you; it's the other guns in the area that triangulate on you and take

---

[112] Base Operations is normally a building on or near the flightline housing flying operations support functions including base weather for pilot weather briefings, a place to gather mission essential information from home units and where pilots file flight plans.

you out while you're holding steady on your target as you come down the chute."

When Ralph engaged a target, he never completely lined up on it until the very last second before firing his guns or dropping his bombs, greatly increasing his survivability on each target run. He also ensured that he varied his egress procedures and routing coming off the target, significantly decreasing the gunners' chances of hitting him. During that mission, the mishap pilot hadn't practiced Ralph's teachings, but he learned his costly lesson and vowed to spread Ralph's message to others.[113]

Second Tour—Fixing Phu Cat

Phu Cat Air Base was strategically located in Southeast Asia for waging tactical warfare. Its northerly position on the east coast of South Vietnam enabled the 12th TFW to be one of the few wings able to fly F-4 tactical sorties in I, II, and III Corps, Laos and Cambodia without air refueling tanker aid. Ralph's wing was able to operate daily into those five locations and deliver its bombs on target wherever needed.[114]

Ralph's drive to return to Vietnam for a second tour was propelled by his desire to continue his push towards more standardization in flight while improving the overall quality of life for his troops at Phu Cat and throughout the war zone. When the opportunity was presented to him to get his own war-time wing in Vietnam, the newlywed jumped at the chance.

---

[113] (R. S. Parr, personal interview)

[114] (R. S. Parr)

Commanding your own wing in the air force, even in peacetime, rarely requires any coercion.

Ralph departed Randolph AFB where he'd been assigned in Rated Officer Assignments, a position responsible for placing flying officers in flying billets around the world. When he showed up for his second tour, the first thing he knew he had to do was, once again, establish his credibility.

He wanted to prove to his people that he, as their new wing commander, had the ability to lead, fly, fight, and win from day one. Greatly reducing the aircraft loss rate during his new command assignment and upcoming one-year deployment at Phu Cat was a prominent goal with an emphasis on quality of life and training while ensuring a seamless transition for people arriving and departing the Southeast Asia (SEA) theatre of operations.[115] All were nearly insurmountable tasks for anyone in Ralph's position.

The operations function of the 12th TFW at Phu Cat was typical of any two-fighter squadron wing. The 389th and 480th Tactical Fighter Squadrons performed exceptionally well under Ralph's leadership. The problems endured during the year were not unique and didn't go unnoticed. A large changeover of personnel during December through February was always painful. The training required for new arrivals to get fully mission ready was completed efficiently in spite of an extremely heavy fragged sortie rate. It's typical of the American 'can do' attitude and certainly reflects the outstanding

---

[115] (R. S. Parr, personal interview)

individual attitude possessed by Ralph's operational personnel.

Ralph worked hard to keep his finger on the pulse of his wing while close observation of the quality of flight leads and instructors was essential even during peaks in fragged missions.

A strong working tactics evaluation shop (Stan/Eval) was a key to successful training. Undoubtedly, the most time-consuming problem of the SEA tour involves the continuous training and indoctrination of newly assigned personnel. Briefings, lectures, policies, publications review, OJT in maintenance, etc., all must be repeated at close intervals. It was estimated that at any one time, there were 20 to 25 percent of his people in training and therefore restricted as to what mission or portion thereof, they may perform. This was a constant problem for all commanders and supervisors. In short, stability in any organization was short lived.

Ralph and his team quickly learned that the solution to this problem was of critical importance if they were to avoid accidents and the resulting combat losses. As a corollary to this problem, it was obvious that some overlap of personnel was required and was of more importance in SEA than in stabilized peace time environments.[116]

Ralph's Phu Cat assignment was interesting throughout but especially from the start. The outgoing Phu Cat Commander was known for his overreactions. They'd lost an airplane during his first week in the country. Ralph learned that they'd actually lost six

---

[116] (R. S. Parr)

airplanes in six weeks. The former commander would stand in front of his troops at squadron meetings and generically say, "We're never gonna do this and never gonna do that and that should clear up these airplane losses." As Ralph prepared to take the reins, the outgoing wing commander told him that in his opinion, there were no changes required in daily operations. Ralph respectfully, yet quietly disagreed. After much discussion, the outgoing commander finally asked Ralph for his thoughts.

Ralph said, "I think we're gonna stop losing so many doggone airplanes when we make a few required procedural changes."

The commander was taken aback at Ralph's response and queried Ralph to clarify his ideas for change. Ralph provided him a thorough, methodical, yet candid response.

Ralph's technical but easily implemented plan called for an increase in the F-4's bomb drop dive angle as you fly down the chute. Using visual aids, including an F-4 model taped to a long wooden stick, he described in detail how he'd increase the dive angle from the currently prescribed 30 degrees to 45 degrees, thus shrinking the impact circle and making the unguided gravity bombs increasingly accurate. The new procedure would enormously decrease the probability of dropping bombs long or short by transforming the bomb's projected impact area from an elliptical pattern to a tighter circular pattern. It is a simple principle that you can demonstrate with a flashlight.

If you hold a flashlight parallel to the floor, then slowly tilt the light to shine onto the floor, you are presented with an elongated area illuminated by your flashlight. As you continue to move the flashlight toward perpendicular to the ground, the ellipse shrinks and becomes a perfect circle when the flashlight is held 90 degrees to the floor or straight down. This principle is still used today in teaching young fighter pilots about the effect that dive angle has on gravity weapons delivery accuracy. Additionally, the pilot reduces the aircraft's exposure to ground fire due to the higher altitude prior to rolling-in, reduced time on the target run, and a higher release altitude prior to egress. Basically, you increase your accuracy while mitigating the risk of an adversary shooting you down throughout the engagement. It was a win-win situation and a concept Ralph lived by.

Ralph also recognized the need to implement new and improved formation tactics. He told the guys to pay close attention to the target you're attacking and especially if multiple passes are required, change your aircraft's attack parameters on each run. By attacking and egressing the target differently each time, it mandates an increase in the pilot's situational awareness on all aircraft in your flight but increases survival odds exponentially. Seventh Air Force Headquarters quickly adopted Ralph's changes, publishing and enforcing them at all bases throughout Vietnam.

Months later, a senior ranking officer from 7th Air Force came back through Phu Cat on a site visit and during a briefing boasted of his theatre-wide improvements and how aircraft loss rates had plummeted since his dive angle changes were implemented.

Ralph quietly stood by, waiting for his opportunity to interject, then said, "I certainly agree with what you've been saying, sir, with one exception."

He said, "What is that?"

Ralph replied, "I was actually the one who initiated the dive angle change and sent it up to 7AF for approval, and you approved and implemented it."

Apparently, he didn't realize that Ralph was a member of the reception party and the one who'd formulated the dive angle plan then pushed the package with improved changes up to his level.

The key to the 45-degree dive angle is that it's more of a visually discernible angle from a pilot's perspective. A pilot doesn't come off the target the same way every time, especially if it's going to take more than one pass to kill the target. A pilot must think like the enemy gunner on the ground and think about the gunner's perspective and realize that his LIMFACS (limiting factors) are in tracking your aircraft. Survivability depends on the pilot's ability to do what it takes to degrade the enemy's targeting solution and the 45-degree dive angle was a perfect start.[117]

Almost all of the 12th Tactical Fighter Wing's missions during the months of May through September 1970 were flown in-country (Vietnam). In October, the number of in-country missions began to decrease as more day and night sorties were fragged out of the country (Laos and Cambodia). Missions supporting in-country operations were flown primarily in direct support of United States Army Forces, Army of the Republic of

---

[117] (R. S. Parr, personal interview)

Vietnam, and other free world forces. In addition to the daily allocation of fragged strike missions, which averaged approximately 25 per day, the 12th TFW maintained eight primary aircraft on alert. In most cases, missions scrambled from the alert pad were employed in emergency situations to support operations such as troops in contact and special forces camps under attack. The alert commitment from April through June 1970 increased to 12 aircraft 24 hours per day when the special forces camps at Dak Pek and Dak Seang were under heavy attack.

Tactical airpower was now given an opportunity to demonstrate its capability as a close air support weapon for defense of friendly positions. The special forces camps of Dak Pek and Dak Seang, located in northwestern II Corps, were besieged by large and determined forces of North Vietnamese Viet Cong. Both camps straddled major infiltration routes and effectively slowed down the flow of men and supplies into South Vietnam. These two actions lasted the entire month of April with peak action coming in the first 10 days, over 178 sorties. Of the two camps, the Dak Seang defense was most critical with 373 sorties necessary to keep the enemy from overrunning the camp.

The support of these two special forces camps proved to be timely and effective. Time after time, the enemy troops were stopped at the perimeter barbed wire by extremely accurate delivery of BLU-27 napalm, MK-82 high-drag bombs and 20-mm cannon fire. To ensure accuracy and because of low ceilings and restricted visibilities, low angle and low altitude deliveries were used. As a result of this exposure and heavy defensive fire from the enemy, it was acknowledged by most pilots to be the heaviest ground fire encountered in South Vietnam.[118]

When the cross-border operations into Cambodia were initiated in May, the 12th TFW out-country commitment shifted almost entirely from Laos to Cambodia. In May, there were 427 Cambodian sorties while in June, there were 361 Cambodian sorties.

Early air strikes into Cambodia were directed mainly against structures, bunker complexes, and fortifications that comprised base camps which had acted as sanctuaries prior to allied operations into Cambodia. These operations were located along the borders of II and III Corps operational areas. The call sign for the former area was Binh Tay while these operations in III Corps used the call word, Toan Thang. A number designator was added to further describe the assigned operation. One of the first areas hit with 20 sorties was the 'Fishhook' northwest of Saigon in support of Operation Toan Thang 43.[119]

Cross-border operations were flown mainly under the same restrictions as those in-country. Being paired to a Forward Air Control (FAC) was mandatory. The fighters were fragged or scrambled to a rendezvous with a FAC who then directed them to specific targets. Later in the campaign when the enemy was forced deeper into Cambodia, the interdiction program started in earnest. The enemy began replacing a shattered infiltration system by using supply lines deeper in the country. This

---

[118] (R. S. Parr, personal interview)

[119] (R. S. Parr)

new system was located in the northeast quarter of Cambodia and included the Mekong River from the Laos's border, south to Krate and then east to Seoul. Rivers branching eastward were also favored lines of communication (LOCs) in addition to the few roads.

As the Binh Tay operations slowed down with the ground units having driven the NVA and Viet Cong back beyond the 29-mile limit set for United States troops, the interdiction war took on the likeness of the air-to-ground war in Laos. By June, only 42 of Binh Tay sorties and 50 Toan Thang sorties were flown compared to the 260 sorties of this type in May. Because of the enemy's control of the waterways, roads, and towns, transshipment and strong points were often located near populated areas. However, under stringent FAC control, boats, docks, ferries, bridges, obvious storage areas hit were Lomphat and Stoeng Treng. Damage to Cambodian towns, villages, and cultural structures was carefully avoided.

From a tactical standpoint, the biggest lesson learned was the fact that we cannot sit idle and allow existing tactics to go too long without reevaluation. Although the basic tactics proved sound, there were areas where modifications were warranted and appropriate.[120]

The constant requirement for refined tactics was because there was so much enemy ground fire on every mission that you could literally see the bullets going by the cockpit as their anti-aircraft guns flooded the sky with bullets. WWII bomber crew members reminisce about the flak being so thick that you could walk on it? Well, in

---

[120] (R. S. Parr)

Vietnam, the ground fire was so thick that it looked like you were flying through a swarm of bees. It was nothing but streams, or sheets, of high-caliber lead coming straight at you on every sortie.

Ralph flew a lot of missions over Laos and also led the first strike in Cambodia when offensive operations opened there. The enemy built roads throughout each country and was running long convoys of vehicles that would operate at night for resupply, then they'd park the vehicles in the jungle under the cover of the forest canopy during the day for seclusion.

After the change in the monsoon season (October), the weather in Laos improved and the in-country weather deteriorated very sharply. This greatly reduced the visual ordnance delivery and troops in contact (TIC) assistance possibility in the Republic of Vietnam. In October 1970, they saw 28.5 inches of rain and in December, 18.7 inches. This drastic shift in weather also shifts the air war to a concentrated effort to reduce the truck flow through the Laotian mountains. In comparison to the July through September quarter of 14 strike missions in Laos, 1,379 were flown from October through December.

The command and control of air power in Laos is very centralized and well controlled. Forces from all F-4 bases in Southeast Asia were tasked against targets within range, even the air refueling range of their aircraft. Though some have suggested specific target area assignment for each base so that F-4 aircrews can be more familiar with the terrain, Ralph didn't feel this was necessary. One major problem Ralph observed was the delay involved with coordinating an air strike after the FAC has discovered a target. This problem was not unique to Laos; it was a standard problem in all areas of SEA; however, due to the control and checking necessary in their present tactics, there was no easy solution.

The coordination and ordnance determination process during Ralph's tour versus a year prior was far superior. Seldom did his pilots arrive and find no FAC or that the ordnance loaded on their aircraft was incorrect for the specific target. When Ralph first arrived nearly 12 months earlier, he saw FACs saturated with strike aircraft and unable to handle each flight due to poor coordination procedures. Whereas at the end of his tour aircraft could divert due to weather changes, etc., and remain effective. Aircraft losses to ground fire decreased significantly through improved indoctrination programs and insistence on safer delivery parameters.

The Tactics/Evaluation Division functioned with more emphasis on evaluation than probably any such organization has in the conduct of the Vietnam War. The emphasis on evaluation rather than standardization was a result of high command guidance and a locally tailored program to overcome the training deficiencies noted in the Replacement Training Unit (RTU) graduates. A separate flight evaluation requirement for the new pilots had shown them to be generally lacking in the ability to recover the aircraft under emergency conditions. The evaluations of front-seat crew members found them poorly trained for any night-time combat activity. They were particularly deficient in their training for acquisition of attacking tactical targets at night.

Another training deficiency was weak preparation for tactics and maneuvers required in the presence of gun defenses. Directly related to this was the lack of knowledge of the capabilities of the normal defense weapons used by communist forces. These deficiencies were overcome by a local indoctrinations program which demanded close evaluation during phase points chosen on the basis of the observed deficiencies in the RTU graduates. This placed a definite training burden upon the combat units as it goes beyond the scope of a local checkout.

A specific weakness in the RTU graduate was a lack of proficiency in delivery of high-drag munitions. Some RTU graduates arrived without ever previously dropping a high-drag bomb. Ralph felt that training programs should recognize that accuracy in low-angle delivery of munitions under combat conditions is largely dependent upon judgment. In contending with target defenses, terrain, and weather conditions, the pilot releasing weapons from low angles will seldom achieve exact computed release conditions.

In addition, the cockpit indications (ADI, altimeter, etc.) are somewhat inaccurate. Pilot judgment based upon visual perceptions was the best means to determine the proper instant to release. This judgment can only be developed by experience, therefore, RTU aircrews should practice with high-drag simulator weapons to properly prepare them for combat employment. The solution of this problem justified the development of a training round that simulates the trajectory of high-drag weapons released from combat parameters.

In the past, it was customary to have formal conferences between the tactical fighter units for the purpose of exchanging information on new tactical concepts and techniques. Ralph knew that the benefits of this program were obvious and the custom should continue.

In tactical operations, there were many proven instances of the need for secure voice (encrypted) communication. Frequently, the response to a clear transmission declaring a specific position at night or an intention to initiate an attack from a stated direction is a large volume of AAA fire. Ralph knew that the enemy listened to our UHF transmissions and would capitalize upon any tactical or intelligence information he can gain.

Ralph didn't have much interaction with chopper pilots and tanker aircrews in theatre unless they happened to land at his base. Air refueling with the KC-135s was very interesting at times, to say the least. Simply combining night-air refueling with a little bad weather and it's a recipe for some heart-wrenching moments in a fuel guzzling F-4C.

A KC-135A refuels an F-4 in contact position.

Ralph hooked up with a tanker one day and was nervous as a long-tailed cat in a room full of rocking chairs because he was 'sucking fumes' as he approached the tanker in the pre-contact position. He needed a contact[121] and the fuel onload, and he needed it now. He was only moments away from flaming out his engines and facing a controlled ejection.

The tanker's boom operator was having a helluva time getting a contact so they could start passing him gas. Ralph had just about enough the boom operator's fumbling around. He was dinging the tip of the nozzle on the spine of Ralph's fuselage so much that Ralph thought that the boom operator was scribing his name. Now even more rattled, Ralph came up on guard (emergency

---

[121] A contact is complete when the tanker and receiver aircraft connect inflight via the tanker's boom and the receiver's receptacle. A teflon seal is made enabling the tanker to transfer fuel to the receiver aircraft.

frequency monitored by all airborne aircraft at the time) and told the tanker to have the boom operator hold the boom steady, and Ralph would facilitate the contact. About that time, the face in the boom pod disappeared and a new, older gentleman's face appeared. *Probably an instructor,* Ralph thought. Thankfully, an immediate contact was complete and Ralph was taking on fuel.

Once he was about half full, Ralph again chimed up on the radio, "Toboggan, toboggan, toboggan!" The tanker immediately started a slow descent while in contact to enable Ralph to stay on the boom. Otherwise, he would have to stroke his afterburner just to stay in contact and continue the fuel transfer. The immediate descent of the tanker and receiver (while in contact), toboggan maneuvers were developed to enable you to trade altitude for airspeed during heavy fuel unloads. This technique was employed extensively in theatre.[122]

Ralph felt that he'd done some good for the average fighter pilot. He would tell them in squadron meetings, "When it's all over, I want you all going home, but while you're here, I want all our missions accomplished in the best, most efficient manner. Please, do what I tell you. And I'm not going to simply tell you; I'll take you out and show you how to do it. Listen to me and we'll get the job done. When you look back at it years later, you'll say to yourself, 'That's the finest flying I've ever done as a professional fighter pilot, even if it was in combat.'"

Ralph was relieved when he was full of fuel again. He thought, *I guess it wasn't my day to punch out and float down to earth in my silk let-down device.*

---

[122] (R. S. Parr, personal interview)

Under strong command guidance, the 12th Tactical Fighter Wing had one of the most effective safety programs in SEA and was able to maintain a record better than the air force average for the F-4. The essence of the wing's safety program is the emphasis on individual responsibility and development of a professional attitude. This was accomplished by an individual interview with each pilot by the deputy commander for operations, the safety officer, unit commander, and operations officer and the wing tactics evaluations officer. Strong emphasis was placed on adherence to wing-flying policies to ensure safety.

As this concept progressed down through the echelons, it resulted in a tight and well-knit organization in which operations were standard and 'by the book', yet flexible enough to develop leadership and professionalism in the individuals. This was only accomplished by exposing each individual to a professional approach from their initial briefing to the last day of their tour. Ralph emphasized the importance of watching the 'old guys' as closely as the new troop. Complacency has no boundaries and Ralph felt that many of our SEA losses were 'old heads' who relaxed their attention to combat and flying basics.

Factors bearing on the safety program were: Nearly all of the sorties flown by the wing involved heavy weight takeoffs, carrying and delivering all types of conventional ordnance in a hostile and hazardous combat environment. The high turnover rate of personnel resulted in the wing continually losing experienced personnel and replacing them mostly with inexperienced personnel.

Phu Cat Air Base had only one runway and a high incidence of crosswinds which were often over 20 knots. Though very low ceilings were infrequent, rain was common place with near flooding conditions during the monsoon seasons.

Maintaining proficiency in a large number of combat tactics, i.e., soft load, hard load, CBU, J-Runs, buff escort, radar bombing, etc., demands flawless training programs. Day/night/bad weather capability in all conventional ordnance with no allowance to specialize also required very strict supervision.

Lessons learned: Ralph didn't sustain an aircraft low blow loss in spite of heavy sortie rates into high threat mountainous areas and attributed this significant improvement to a reevaluation of their ordnance delivery parameters and ensuing change in wing policies. By keeping the pilots 'out of the weeds' and teaching them to deliver at safer altitudes, the combat safety record improved immensely and sacrificed nothing in continuance of an outstanding tactical air support record.

Ralph said that Phu Cat Air Base was the finest base in the Republic of Vietnam (RVN). Being the last base constructed, its growth pace was slightly hampered by austerity in construction funds. It was functionally well laid out and regarded as the most attractive in RVN. The progress of construction during the late 60s was continuous and while some of the 'nice to have' facilities were lacking, when Ralph arrived, they became a reality, boosting morale.

Officers and enlisted clubs, swimming pool, air-conditioned theatre, library, tennis courts, golf facilities, hobby shops, and many other special services were consistently rated outstanding. At Phu Cat, where to be off-base was off-limits, a greater priority was given early in the construction program to emphasize 'people' facilities.

Drug Abuse

The drug abuse problem for those serving in Vietnam received vast attention and became a politically sensitive issue. The medical profession became a false hope by permitting the public to think that it can develop appropriate medical diagnosis and medical cures for such sociological ills as a breakdown in American family life and parental responsibilities, and the lack of a culturally acquired discipline and responsibility beyond the self. In spite of the ready availability of marijuana and heroin in Vietnam, Ralph believed that there would be no drug problem among the American military in Vietnam if one had not either tolerated or was at least present in the CONUS. It was difficult to see how the trend toward greater compassion in the courts and forgiving laxity toward the individual will strengthen any military unit in which these egocentric and irresponsible individuals were found in Vietnam or anywhere else. Ralph said that there was no way an amnesty program would have strengthened our air power in SEA, for this air power ultimately depends more upon the quality of the man than the quality of the aircraft.

To accomplish the job of wing commander, the natural desire was to select an outstanding staff. In Southeast Asia, this was really more than a desire; it was a necessity, and Ralph was truly blessed with such high caliber personnel. His people often worked seven days a week, 15 hours a day, to get the job done. It was always accomplished just that way and Ralph applauded their dedication. Without question, being commander of the 12th Tactical Fighter Wing was Ralph's most exciting and rewarding assignment and he was particularly proud to have had the opportunity to command the 'Fighting Twelfth'.[123]

---

[123] (R. S. Parr)

Chapter 12
Risky Iran

The Iranian oil industry developed rapidly in the 1920s with production more than quadrupling over the course of the decade—with British capital dominating the sector. It was the nationalization of the oil industry by Prime Minister Mohammed Mosadeq in 1951 that prompted his removal in a coup instigated by the Central Intelligence Agency (CIA) two years later. The toppling of Mosadeq's nationalist and secular democratic government allowed Reza Shah's son, Mohammed Reza, to consolidate his autocratic rule—and then to accelerate the modernization project.

The post-coup era, notably the 1960s and 1970s, saw remarkable economic growth—with rates averaging 11 percent annually from 1963 to 1972 and jumping to 30 percent during 1974 and 1975. Oil income financed extensive programs of industrialization, national education, and urban development, while land reforms enhanced capitalist relations in the countryside, curtailing the power of feudal lords and turning the peasantry into smallholders or rural proletarians, many of whom subsequently migrated to the cities. In the course of this historic shift, modern classes—professionals and technocrats, the working class, women in public roles—

rose to prominence at the expense of the traditional social structure and forms of authority: the feudal class, bazaar merchants, the lemma, and Islamic institutions in general.[124]

Tehran became the spatial embodiment of this surging accumulation process. In and around the city, industry, commerce, services, and foreign enterprises mushroomed. More than a place of production, Tehran became a site of ever-increasing consumption, as new spending patterns and Western lifestyles were adopted; restaurants, cafes, and exclusive uptown neighborhoods appeared. The Shah's regime sought to reshape Tehran into a decentered, Los Angeles-type suburban entity.

The first comprehensive plan of Tehran, drawn up by the Californian architect Victor Gruen in 1963 thru 1967, envisioned a city divided into ten large and fairly self-contained districts of 500,000 inhabitants, linked to one another through a network of freeways and a rapid transportation system. This postmodern plan, however, failed to account for what had amounted to Iran's 'enclosure movement' of the 1960s and 1970s: the land-reform program had effectively released some three million landless peasants from the countryside. They looked to the cities, primarily Tehran, to rebuild their lives. Mass rural-urban migration swelled the capital's population, contributing to its virtual doubling from 2.7 million in 1965 to 4.6 million in 1975.[125]

The new arrivals were predominantly poor, but it was urban planning and the zoning policy that turned them

---

[124] (Bayat) 155

[125] (Bayat) 166

into 'marginals' (hashiyenishinan). The free market in land and its high price, as well as problems of cost and the restrictive construction—all pushed poor newcomers to put up their shelters informally, outside the city limits. Underdog neighborhoods such as Shahbaz Jonoubi, Javadieh, Naziabad, and Biseem-e-Najafabad sprang up, occupied mainly by rural migrants.

Housing supply had previously been tight in the mid-1950s, more than half of all households in Tehran lived in rented homes, and some 40 percent, mostly rural migrants, lived in one or two rooms. By the 1970s, some 200,000 new homes were needed every year to keep up with the demand. The shortage of supply would only expand the slums, squatter settlements, and satellite communities around the city.[126]

There were huge cultural differences unbeknownst to Ralph. The first that came to Ralph's mind was that the Iranians worked at different speeds than Americans did. While the Iranian hostage crisis was still seven years away, Ralph absorbed every bit of historical information, including how the overall Iranian literacy rate was improving rapidly, and middle management techniques were in revision—Ralph would soon receive a crash course in all of the above.

Ralph was the director of safety at Headquarters United States Air Forces Europe (USAFE) in the summer of 1972, when he found out that Pentagon officials had requested him by name for immediate reassignment as chief of staff of the Military Air Advisory Group (MAAG) in Tehran, Iran. Being totally unfamiliar with

---

[126] (Bayat) 156

the requirements of the position, Ralph anticipated an extremely steep learning curve during the handover process. The job was not physically located at the American Embassy in Tehran, but in an adjacent complex, however, he constantly had a pulse on actions taking place within the embassy.[127]

As the chief of staff, he worked in the air section for the chief of the MAAG, a position held by a two-star army general. They also had navy and army sections. One thing that Ralph immediately noticed in Iran was that people bought cars based on how much car they could afford. The more money you had, the faster, more glamorous car you owned. There were hazards that accompany that approach.

A person's automobile didn't always match, and often exceeded the driving capability of the person behind the wheel. The roadways were a free-for-all as he found that no two cars drove at the same speed. Patience, or lack thereof, may have played a role in the NASCAR-like race environment or it could have simply been poor time management, but it seemed that somebody always wanted to pass you.

One day, something captured Ralph's attention in his rear-view mirror. The same car was tailing him during the majority of his drive into work. The car changed lanes, matching his lane changes and followed every turn he made, so he immediately reported the suspicious activity to the security people when he arrived at the office. The leadership immediately assigned Ralph four permanent body guards who worked in two-man shifts.

---

[127] (R. S. Parr, personal interview)

They were well-trained and took very good care of Ralph. They walked with him down the street and when he wanted to go into a local store, one would watch the door, while the other guard went inside to inspect the safety aspects of the store prior to his entrance.[128]

It was a very intense time, even with body guard protection. Ralph was hosting a cocktail party one night at their home for some high-ranking Iranian military officers. As the night wore on, his security officers entered his house, informing Ralph that a letter bomb was discovered in his mailbox during the party. The mailbox was built into a seven-foot tall security wall around the perimeter of his house, which was displaced away from the main road forming his own mini compound for security purposes.

The outside perimeter of Ralph's house appeared even safer because the Shah's palace, fortified with heavily armed guards, was directly across the street, so those security forces could see Ralph's entire property and provide firepower, if required. The letter bomb was quickly and safely removed by military explosives experts but raised a lot of eyebrows. Ralph had no idea if the bomb was planted there by someone at the cocktail party or by someone on the outside—a simple fact he would never know for sure.

A few days later and a short distance across an open field from his house, a man was spotted covertly running in a circular pattern near Ralph's property. Ralph had no idea what this guy's intentions were but again, Ralph's personal security forces were further strengthened,

---

[128] (R. S. Parr, personal interview)

including more manning to bolster the available firepower, countering the increased perceived threat.

Ralph didn't feel safe at all. His wife, Margaret, was back in the States, visiting her daughter who was graduating from college at the time. Margaret didn't care much for her time spent in Iran during his assignment either as they always had to be on the defensive with an eye on situational awareness around the clock. Ralph could see his protective chase-car lagging approximately 50 to 75 yards behind him during every commute to and from work. They were just far enough back to remain as stealthy as possible.[129]

One day, a Jeep rapidly approached Ralph's car from behind. As it pulled out to pass Ralph's staff car, he pulled up right beside, matching the staff car's speed. Ralph slowly turned his head to look directly across at the man sitting in the right rear seat of the Jeep. Then he saw the right front passenger; both passengers were armed with Thompson sub-machine guns with their muzzles aimed directly at Ralph. No shots were fired as engine roar of his chase car countered all other traffic noise as it pulled in tight behind him, attempting to crowd the Jeep away from Ralph's vehicle. The Jeep was forced to jump the curb veering into a self-made cloud of sand and dust as it fled across an open field with its heavily armed occupants holding on for dear life.

---

[129] (R. S. Parr, personal interview)

Thompson Sub-Machine Gun

Later that week, Ralph's executive officer was shot to death as he was leaving the front door of his house to catch a staff car ride to work. An assassin stepped out from behind the corner building and shot him in the back of the head as the young, up and coming officer walked past. The day after Ralph's Executive Officer was killed, his Iranian staff car driver said, "Now, I understand why you take a different route to and from work every day." A simple morning commute had transformed into a major stressor in Ralph's life.

Ralph's time in Iran was extremely dangerous; something he was aware of going into the job because the history of folks holding his position was not very good. The guy he replaced was hit by a bomb before Ralph was tagged for his position. The blast didn't immediately kill him, however, he passed away a couple of years later. Then, the guy who replaced Ralph and his driver were shot to death by machine guns while driving to work in their staff car. That's why Ralph wanted to dissuade anyone who was tracking him from pinning any routine activities on him. It was a risky assignment. Margaret was afraid for the entire year-and-a-half long tour. Going home to be with her daughter was the best thing for her.

Ralph's time in Iran was an assignment he'd like to forget but the lessons he learned regarding risk mitigation would stick with him for the next 40 years.[130]

---

[130] (R. S. Parr, personal interview)

Chapter 13
Unsuspecting Fall Finale

A man known as the father of English literature and a poet of the middle ages spouted an eight-word quote in 1374 that 602 years later could not better sum up one day in Ralph's life.

"All good things must come to an end."

--Geoffrey Chaucer

The quote spread to the United States and altered with some additional words around 1680.

Ralph felt fortunate to have enjoyed two assignments in Florida, separated by a few years. Both jobs were very rewarding. MacDill and Eglin AFBs each had a lot to offer and cast fond memories for Ralph and Margaret to last a lifetime as they together experienced the highest of highs and lowest of lows.

Having just returned from their assignment in Iran, he and Margaret were elated to be heading stateside to MacDill AFB, Florida, for their next assignment and the challenges they'd encounter beyond the horizon.

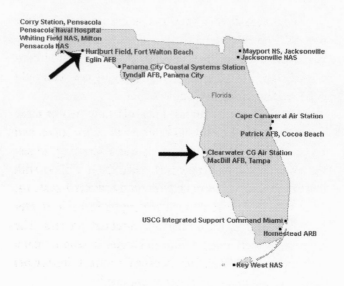

First F-4 Squadron

Ralph was lucky enough to be considered, then selected to stand up the first F-4 squadron in the air force. Ralph was slated to stand up an F-4 outfit complete with a squadron commander plus four other initial cadre pilots. Pete 'Speedy' Everett was the first F-4 squadron commander, and he was a good one.[131] It's always difficult setting up a squadron from scratch, but each did his part to make it come to fruition. Ralph earned the

---

[131] (R. S. Parr, personal interview)

distinction of becoming the first instructor pilot in the F-4.

They were flying Navy F-4Bs during the checkout process. The B-model aircraft sported beefed up landing gear able to absorb the jaw-wrenching shock of aircraft carrier landings, even though they were currently employed as land-based trainers.

Early on in the process, the DoD flew two or three test pilots down from the F-4 factory to check Ralph and his buddies out in the aircraft. It was interesting, to say the least. Ralph and his peers shocked the test pilots with their innate ability to quickly learn the aircraft systems, then put the aircraft through the rigors of basic fighter maneuvers, or BFM, during the checkout process. The debriefings were normally much shorter in length than a wartime sortie debriefing because contract instructors rarely had anything to debrief or critique.[132]

It was a rather hectic time in our country's political realm. The Russians had recently placed missiles and other weaponry on the island of Cuba, raising the eyebrows of many, especially in the Kennedy Administration and Pentagon leadership. It drove the formation of a division command at MacDill operational in less than a month before the Cuban Missile Crisis.

On October 14, 1962, two USAF U-2s photographed portions in Cuba, revealing Soviet offensive nuclear missiles based only 90 miles from United States shores. President John F. Kennedy placed U.S. forces on alert, and USAF U-2 and RF-101 reconnaissance flights over Cuba continued, the latter aircraft sometimes flying at

---

[132] (R. S. Parr, personal interview)

treetop level. On October 22, President Kennedy publicly announced details of the critical situation and ordered a naval blockade of Cuba.

Meanwhile, USAF aircraft kept the island and surrounding waters under constant surveillance, providing the United States Navy with data on scores of ships at sea, apparently en route to Cuba. On October 27, USAF Maj. Rudolf Anderson Jr. was shot down and killed while flying a U-2 mission over Cuba. The superpowers inched even closer to war. The next day, Soviet Premier Nikita Khrushchev—faced with United States resolve to prevent Soviet strategic weapons being placed so close to the United States—agreed to remove the offensive missiles as well as medium range bombers being assembled in Cuba. USAF U-2s and RF-101s then monitored communist compliance in removing this threat to American security.[133]

Once the F-4 squadron was up and operational, the personnel center had put Ralph on orders to move to Randolph AFB in San Antonio, Texas. The formation of the division command swamped the personnel center with numerous billets to fill at MacDill, so in Ralph's mind, one easy fill was to pull him off his PCS orders to Randolph AFB and keep him at MacDill, saving two permanent changes of station or moves (him leaving and them moving in his replacement) to serve in the newly formed unit. The wing commander called him in and said, "You're gonna run my command post here at MacDill." The move to San Antonio was off.

---

[133] (Cuban Missile Crisis)

At the time, Ralph didn't even know what a command post was. He had just come out of a MAAG in a foreign country, but as usual, he saluted smartly and took on the new position with eyes wide open, ready and willing to do what was right for the air force.

Once he settled into the chief of the command post position, he took his duties extremely seriously. The division commander entered the secure command post one day with another officer close in tow. Ralph presented them with his routine command post tour, then the commander and his side kick departed. The visitor who had trailed his commander happened to come back alone after lunch but soon found that he couldn't get past the secure entrance. A young enlisted troop met him at the sealed door and wouldn't allow him past the cipher locked door.

After a little one-sided discussion with Ralph's troop, the visitor barked, "Get the command post director out here."

So, Ralph's enlisted troop made his way back to Ralph's office to inform him of what had transpired at the door. Ralph quickly got up from his desk and meandered his way through the long, dark, and secluded hallway and approached the door to meet the visitor. The returning visitor was just 'a little peeved' that he wasn't allowed to enter. Voices became louder as Ralph and the visitor went round and round, when the visitor finally said, "Well, I need to get some information off the big board in there."

Ralph replied, "I'm sorry, but you don't have clearance." Ralph was a major at the time and the visitor, a full-bird colonel.

As he attempted to pull rank on Ralph, he semi-screamed, "Don't tell me I can't come in there because I bloody well can."

Ralph quickly replied, "Well, you can't right now."

"We'll see about that," he said, and he left in a quick cantor for his staff car and sped away. As Ralph turned to head back to his desk, he smiled at his young troop who'd listened to the entire conversation from afar and Ralph said, "Good job, son."

Later that afternoon, a staff car pulled up, driven by the same individual, but this time, he had the division commander with him. The division commander had a big grin on his face as he punched the cipher lock code and came through the big steel door. The visitor wasn't smiling one bit and, in fact, carried a frown on his face. He wasn't masking how pissed off he really was at Ralph and the whole situation, at all.

Ralph's commander said, "I've authorized him to enter, so he can get the information he needs."

Ralph said, "Yes sir," and let them enter.

As the now escorted 'visitor' walked past, he turned to Ralph and said, "You'd better hope you never have to work for me."

Ralph, somewhat taken aback, stopped him in his tracks and said, "Sir, if I ever have to work for you, at least you'll know that I'll follow my boss' orders," and things were peaceful after that.

President Kennedy arrives at MacDill AFB, FL
18 November 63

Ralph's command post assignment enabled him to witness events never to be seen from the cockpit. Sometime later, Ralph was sitting at his desk and just happened to look outside as a procession of people paraded by his window. Lo and behold, President Kennedy walked by as he was headed out to his airplane to depart the base. He'd flown into MacDill AFB, the current home of U.S. Strike Command to speak on the Cuban situation before a large crowd at Al Lopez Stadium in Tampa, Florida, just a few days before he was assassinated in Dallas. The news of his assassination on 22 November 1963 hit Ralph a little extra hard, knowing he'd just seen him the day before. Ralph's secretary simply dissolved when she heard that the president had been shot.[134]

---

[134] (R. S. Parr, personal interview)

Medically Retired

Ralph's second assignment to Florida occurred in the mid-1970s. Although the assignment was an awesome job, it would prove to mark the end of his historic career.

He was the Chief of Staff of the Armament Development and Test Center responsible for some 670 square miles plus the ranges where weapons test sorties were flown. A horrifying storm came through one day and in only a few short seconds, it ripped 19 trees from Ralph and Margaret's beautiful property.

As a result of the storm, a couple of trees fell on Ralph's house. He decided that he'd better get up there to remove the trees from the roof, inspect, and patch any holes. Ralph was an O-6 and could have (should have) had housing maintenance come look at the storm damage situation, but his type-A personality (the 'I can fix anything' mentality) kicked in.

He retrieved his ladder from the garage and leaned it against the awning on the house. He safely climbed onto the roof and began the task at hand. He happened to lean over to check one gouge in a shingle that was near the lower edge of a valley in the roof line. As he leaned over, a pair of sunglasses fell out of his breast pocket. In what seemed like slow motion, they hung in flight, right in front of his face. Instinctively, he quickly reached out to snatch them. Things literally went downhill from there.

His quick movements made him lose his balance on the sloped roof, forcing him to take a big step backward, attempting to regain his balance. Finding no 'big step' of roof available, his big toe was the only part of his body to catch the edge of the roof, then it too slipped from the edge and away he went for the ride of his life, backward.

He went head first; his body weaving its way through the rungs of the aluminum ladder, his unprotected head not missing a step, before his now limp body cascaded onto the concrete driveway. He'd fallen more than 12 feet, broken his back in two places and broke his neck, again. He'd previously broken his neck in a fall from a banister years before.

Hearing from inside what sounded like a meteor hitting the roof, Margaret came rushing out to help him up.

Ralph said, "Don't touch me."

He knew that his injuries were serious because all he could feel was the sensation of pins sticking into his body from head to toe. He told Margaret to call the base leadership to inform them what had happened and to have them immediately send an ambulance to rush him to the hospital. Thank God, the ambulance was there in no time, thus beginning an extremely long medical process. The healing process was something he never wanted to experience again.

He suffered through six back and neck surgeries over the years. After a couple of fusions, he was as fixed as he was ever going to be.

That was 1975, and he was medically retired from the air force in 1976. Since then, he spent a lot of time in the hospital and did not work another job after he left the military.

During his fifth spinal surgery, they opened him up and basically rebuilt his pelvis and lower back with titanium. About six weeks later, he went in for a checkup, and they discovered that his body was rejecting the titanium. That forced a sixth surgery and subsequent bone graft with cadaver bone to replace the titanium in order to reverse his body's rejection. Those were very tough times in Ralph's life as he learned that this invincible fighter pilot wasn't so invincible after all and that, indeed, all good things do come to an end.

Chapter 14
Eight Years Earlier—Re-attack

Ralph was oblivious to the fact that his air-force career would come to a screeching halt in eight short years. Not as a result of enemy gun or missile fire or heaven forbid, an aircraft mishap, but medically retired over a pair of sunglasses. Subconsciously, he'd wondered now and then how it would all end, but today, he was purely focused on silencing those mortar and gun positions around Khe Sanh and safely returning him, McManus, and their F-4 back to safety.

Ralph stole another quick glance out the right side and could still see the North Vietnamese Army (NVA) gunners' bullets race towards his F-4. The battle damage that he and McManus had sustained on the previous target runs and the marine battalion commander's desire for them to depart the target area would not be enough to end this engagement.

With one dry pass and four successful napalm passes resulting in two dead mortar positions, Ralph and Tom would continue the attack on the remaining NVA gun emplacements with the only offensive weapon remaining on the jet, the 20-mm external gun. Unbeknownst to either man, fuel, or the lack thereof, was weighing heavy on each of their minds. Time was critical as they soon would be forced to depart the area to either hit an air refueling tanker for a top off or RTB (return to base).[135]

Leading up to the 16 March 1968 mission at Khe Sanh, it was reported that there had been two American KIAs on 13 March, two on the 14th and one on the 15th.[136]

The main U.S. goal in the Southeast Asia War was to protect South Vietnam—initially from a local communist insurgency and later from conquest by communist North Vietnam. The U.S. also hoped to prevent the spread of communism to other nearby countries. Although popularly known as the Vietnam War, U.S. efforts included military action not only in South and North Vietnam but also in neighboring Southeast Asian countries.[137]

The 1,000 to 1,200 rounds per second targeting the F-4 seemed to Ralph and Tom like they were a magnet for 10 times that amount. Ralph told the FAC that he would continue making gun passes until he was out of ammo or gas due to the high priority 7AF placed on finding and destroying those guns. The FAC found himself precariously caught in the middle as he wanted his buddies on the ground safe, but not at the expense of Parr's and McManus' lives. The FAC anxiously cleared Ralph in for the next pass. Ralph flew fast and low, and

---

[135] McManus would remember, "Years later, Ralph and I discussed our dire fuel state during the engagement but each of us was so focused on silencing the remaining guns that neither mentioned it over the intercom in the jet."

[136] (Mannion)

[137] (The Southeast Asia War: Vietnam, Laos and Cambodia)

feverishly worked to maintain visual on the target. He was more likely to slam his aircraft into the ground than not. It was dangerous and nearly impossible to see what was happening below; it was simply all a blur, but it was the only way he could get close enough to the target for effective gun passes. Losing visibility on the target area was a risk, but so was getting shot to pieces. The cloud and smoke layers were even lower now, further hindering visibility in the target area.

Ralph pulled hard on the stick as he swung his aircraft around the pattern again. Entering in and out of the enemy's fire control envelope, he could see that the ammo tracers were tracking his aircraft at a faster pace with each pass. It was coming up in sheets. He flashed back to when he was a kid and his friend would point the water hose at him. He could see every droplet of water squirting directly at him in slow motion. Only now, it wasn't water—it was direct enemy gun fire.

He continued his target runs, firing his 20-mm gun until he ran out of ammunition. Finally, Ralph had put the enemy guns out of action by totally destroying the gun emplacements as a result of his pounding passes.

The battalion commander soon relayed via the FAC's radio congratulations to Ralph and Tom for making it out of there alive. He said that he was impressed with their determination.

Parr and McManus headed back to Cam Ranh Bay. After landing, with their nerves a little on edge and thoughts slightly scrambled, they quickly climbed out of the Phantom as ground crews immediately began working on the aircraft in preparation for its next mission. Parr's aircraft had taken a direct hit through the lower right side of the fuselage that had passed through exiting out the left side of the aircraft. Parr and McManus walked around the aircraft, surveying the battle damage. Counting 27 holes, they couldn't believe that they'd safely made it back to the base with the mid fuselage ripped wide open.[138]

The idea of pushing Medal of Honor paperwork was bounced around the air force wing leadership including the new wing commander. Ralph had known him for some time and they had never seen eye-to-eye.[139]

The wing commander didn't realize that Ralph's roommate was his deputy, so he had no idea that Ralph would hear what the commander was saying about Ralph around the office.

The deputy told Ralph the commander's first comment after seeing the Medal of Honor paperwork was, "Jesus Christ, Parr's been here 10 days and doesn't even have a DFC (Distinguished Flying Cross) yet."

Once Ralph heard that the commander had said those words in the office, it was a moot point. The squadron leadership attempted to persuade the wing commander into submitting the Medal of Honor paperwork. He said that he had no feelings either way on the matter.

---

[138] Both Parr and McManus confirmed (in separate interviews) that each had counted 27 holes in their Phantom. An in-depth search for the crew chief of F-4 tail #640726 as a third confirmation of the battle damage turned up empty.
[139] (Parr)

Somewhat compromising, the commander then said, "I'll approve the Air Force Cross," which was a downgrade from the Medal of Honor.[140]

He had the Air Force Cross paperwork resubmitted to his office. It sat in the commander's inbox for months until he left for another assignment.[141] That's when the next wing commander moved in and sent the paperwork forward in an attempt to take care of unfinished business. The Air Force Cross paperwork made its way up the chain for final approval. Ralph stayed out of it. After all, he wasn't out there risking his life for medals. He felt this was his job and took it very seriously.

The NVA pulled out a couple weeks later after suffering heavy B-52 bombing and even more tactical air strikes from fighter aircraft.

The allies had applied an incredible amount of firepower upon the North Vietnamese. Tactical aircraft and B-52s flew 24,449 sorties in support of Khe Sanh, dropping 103,500 tons of ordnance. The artillerymen of the 1st Battalion, 13th Marines and the 2nd Battalion, 94th Field Artillery fired 102,660 rounds of various calibers at enemy positions.[142]

---

[140] (McManus)

[141] (McManus) McManus would speculate, "There may still have been some negative feelings towards Ralph over the IL-12 shootdown in Korea that carried on for many years. That could be why Ralph's Medal of Honor paperwork was shot down and the reason he was never promoted beyond Colonel."

[142] (Shulimson) 283

The North Vietnamese, in turn, fired 10,908 rounds of artillery, mortars, and rockets into U.S. positions in and around Khe Sanh. This fire, combined with small-unit action from Operation Scotland, beginning on 1 November 1967, caused the deaths of 205 defenders of Khe Sanh. Another 1,668 fell wounded, about half of them serious enough to require evacuation.[143]

The NVA had hammered the camp for more than 70 days. Once Ralph had dispensed his napalm and switched to gun passes, the impressed airborne FAC started calling Ralph 'Sir' over the radios rather than using his call sign.

During the engagement, the FAC had said, "You're hitting the targets that we previously couldn't find. We've lost numerous aircraft by those two enemy mortars and four quad anti-aircraft guns and you silenced them in a single F-4 sortie."

The first page of the two-page post-mission report filed by Major Edward D. Silver, the pilot of the second Phantom in Ralph's flight, details the actions of both aircraft during the engagement that day.[144] It should be noted that the two hits Parr and McManus took are addressed on page one. It states that Parr took one hit in the left wing which creased the bottom of the wing. He also took one hit in the centerline that penetrated the oxygen air door and exited after ricocheting off the ejection gun for the ejection seat. The 12th TFW Association Historian said that it was customary for

---

[143] (Shulimson) 283

[144] No detailed information regarding Major Edward D. Silver and Lt. Col. Ernest Craigwell's portion of the mission is available as Silver was KIA on a subsequent mission on 5 July 1968 and Craigwell passed away in April, 2011.

personnel responsible for drafting medal paperwork for sorties like Ralph's to detach page two of the post-mission report for use in generating the medal citation paperwork to send forward for consideration.[145]

---

[145] (Malayney) According to 12th TFW Assn. Historian, Norman Malayney, page two the post-mission report would have described in great detail the remaining battle damage to Parr's aircraft and would have accounted for the 27 holes in the jet. He has perused numerous Vietnam post-mission reports where this was the case.

Parr's 9 passes on 16 March 68 sortie

1. Dry pass (No weapons released)
2. Napalm drop
3. Napalm drop
4. Napalm drop
5. Napalm drop
6. Gun pass
7. Gun pass
8. Gun pass
9. Gun pass

Several years later, Ralph's step-daughter, Linda, was working her way through college as a waitress at a bar along the river in Austin, Texas. As usual, after the business closed for the night, the staff went for a drink before they headed for home. It was late, or early depending on how you look at the time, but she said that this guy, a Vietnam Vet, stood up to tell a story about Khe Sanh and the unforgettable event he'd witnessed. He said that he was one of the marines standing on the ground at the base of a hill, watching this F-4C in action one day. He said that he stood and watched the whole show.

As Linda told Ralph the story, he remembered flying in the pattern for every gun pass, remembering those C-130 aircrew members who'd died from the firepower unleashed by the gunners. They would wait till the C-130 was low, slow, and barely airborne, then they'd open fire on them. The large, slow cargo aircraft were easy prey as they made the turn on departure.

Ralph had a vendetta on those guns. He and the 7AF leadership knew that those guns had to go. Ralph strategically set up his patterns to strafe lengthwise across the target area. If he missed one emplacement, his stream of bullets might rain down on others during each pass. Ralph further increased his probability of survival by not fully lining up on the target until the last second. That, coupled with flying 'out of the sun' hindered the enemy's visibility and, more importantly, ability to target his aircraft. On a couple of passes, they failed to even get a shot off.[146]

---

[146] (McManus)

During one pass, he was so close to the guns that Ralph looked out the side of his aircraft and saw the gunner's mouth wide open.[147]

Linda said that the marine didn't know who that son-of-a-bitch was in the F-4, but he was sure glad that he was on his side.

She said to the marine, "I've heard that story somewhere before."

He replied, "You couldn't have because I've never talked much about it." He had witnessed this incredible display of airmanship evolve from ground level. When she told him that her stepdad WAS that guy up there in the F-4, he nearly went into cardiac arrest.

They make up idioms for a reason, and to say that Ralph remembered it as clear as a bell is not a lie. At the age of 88, health failing due to cancer, Ralph said that it was like driving a car through a swarm of bumblebees. You could literally see the non-tracers flying past the cockpit. It was a blur to your visual senses. In the days following Ralph's Khe Sanh sortie, there were no American KIAs on 16 or 17 March, two on 18 March and none on 19 March.[148]

What started as a small U.S. program to train the South Vietnamese army in 1961 grew into a massive military effort. U.S. combat operations began in South Vietnam and eventually spread to North Vietnam, Laos and Cambodia. The increasing U.S. commitment aimed

---

[147] Ralph remembered thinking, "Jesus, I can see silver in his teeth!" Parr, Ralph S. personal interview. 30 November 2011

[148] (Mannion)

to combat local communist insurgents, North Vietnamese troops, and the flow of supplies supporting them.[149]

McManus had Parr's back throughout the entire engagement. Even though Ralph took the lead, McManus was with him all the way and Ralph knew that Tom would hang with him. During the climb out and on the way home, McManus calmly pressed his push-to-talk switch on his stick for the intercom. Nearly whispering into Ralph's helmet, he asked, "Well, were my balls brass enough, sir?"

Ralph chuckled and said, "You did fine, Tom. I was just a little too distracted to hold a discussion with you at the time." They both knew that they had to nurse their wounded Phantom back to base and live to fly another day.

From that day forward, they talked on the phone from time to time until Ralph passed away. A friendship for life was born that day, March 16, 1968.

---

[149] (The Southeast Asia War: Vietnam, Laos and Cambodia)

Chapter 15
Short String

Ralph lived a very good life. He felt that we all are 'issued a certain length of string', mentally clipping portions of our string as we face the trials and tribulations of life. People utilize their string in different ways and at varying rates. He felt that it is imperative to use your string in the best ways possible in order to make the world a better place as we meander through life's journey.

Take for instance the military and the nomadic lifestyle it instills in all its family members. A two- or three-year assignment cycle forces numerous families to move more than 10 times during a 20 to 30-year career, but it was implemented years ago for a reason.

Most of us are 'fixers' and gain an intense fulfillment of satisfaction in leaving something better than it was before we got it. That mindset lays the foundation and is the backbone of leaders, managers, and commanders of organizations at all levels, even at the entry-level. The desire to constantly improve the robust policies, procedures, and techniques is why our military is the best in the world. Obviously, huge strides in technological advancements play a key role as well. But no matter the capabilities of each individual, the military, in effect, forces improvement in all facets and at all levels as time goes on and this same philosophy works in the civilian sector as well.

The most important job you have is the one you currently hold. You may not like the position or the duties it fulfills, but your ability to enhance processes and implement improvements will make you shine, greasing the skids for your next position, which just may include a promotion. It works from the least common denominator through the highest-ranking leader in any organization. As a leader, the most important aspect in your job is taking care of your people. Ralph witnessed the effects of this more times than he could count during his 34-year air force career.[150]

He recalled at one of the personnel center staff meetings, his director of air force policy on assignments told Ralph, "Colonel, you can't play God."

Ralph replied, "Oh, yes, I can. If I see a guy who, by no fault of his own, is having family problems due to unforeseen circumstances and he's done well up to that point, I'm going to help him out in his next assignment."

He said, "What if the boss finds out?"

Ralph said, "Hell, I'll tell him." At the staff meeting that afternoon, he back briefed his boss about an unpopular assignment decision he was facing that day and his plan to fix the problem via the officer's follow-on assignment. The director witnessed the verbal exchange and was stunned at Ralph's forthcoming attitude during the conversation with his boss.

---

[150] (R. S. Parr, personal interview)

The boss said, "That's why I put you in that position, Ralph." [151]

Being totally up front and honest with his boss during his desk job at the personnel center opened an entirely new door in Ralph's career. When his personnel assignment was winding down, he told the boss, "Here I am, a full colonel and a bachelor . . . I need to volunteer to go back to Vietnam." [152]

As a result of his candidness and taking care of people, the boss told Ralph, "I'll send you back to Vietnam and put you in a wing leadership position over there," and he did. Ralph went back to Vietnam, this time as wing commander at Phu Cat, which ended up being one of the best assignments Ralph ever had.

He was asked on numerous occasions since his retirement in 1976 to rank order his favorite aircraft that he had flown and why. Ralph flew so many different airplanes that he narrowed it down to his top four:

The P-38 was his favorite, as it had great power and excellent turn rate. It had excellent maneuverability and was simply a joy to fly.

The F-86 introduced simplified flying. It was a fighter pilot's dream at the time. It almost responded to what you were thinking before you put control inputs into place to start a turn or maneuver. It was also an excellent gun platform.

---

[151] (R. S. Parr, personalinterview)

[152] That was shortly before he and Margaret were married. Ralph actually returned to Vietnam as a newlywed after he and Margaret were married at the Randolph AFB Chapel in 1969.

The F-4 was sort of a stepchild. It was a gas hog but had an awful lot of power. A funny story about the F-4 involved a McDonnell Douglas test pilot who'd come to check Ralph out as the first F-4 Instructor Pilot in the front seat at MacDill. The ride went very well, and as he proudly stepped out of 'his' jet, he said, "Well, Ralph! How'd you like the jet? Are there any possible improvements you could wish for?"

Ralph nonchalantly responded, "More power!" The instructor's eyes grew big as he damn near buckled at his knees in response to Ralph's reply. The overarching feeling of every fighter pilot is power converts to speed and speed is life.

The P-51 had excellent power and maneuverability. Ralph flew it in two or three places in Japan and the U.S. The P-51 was the number-one fighter for a long time, prior to the jet age. [153]

It amazed Ralph at the enormous technological advancements in aviation and the associated aerial accomplishments made over the past 100 years. The aviation advancements witnessed since the Wright brothers flew were simply mind boggling to him. Ralph relied on machine guns and his eyeballs to acquire and take out an enemy aircraft back in the day. Now, we have a four-ship of F-22 Raptors or F-35 Lightning aircraft receiving time sensitive data via many means, providing the pilots with a God's-eye view of the battlefield below and airspace above.

A pilot now has complete and constant situational awareness through high-resolution displays at his/her

---

[153] (R. S. Parr, personal interview)

fingertips. As a world superpower, we need to continue capitalizing on the thoughts and innovations of all engineers, especially the younger ones in order to completely capture the unending available technological advancements. The sky truly is the limit.[154]

The advent of remotely piloted aircraft, or RPAs, is a whole new realm and we've simply scratched the surface on what is to come.

We can't afford to stiff arm, or even worse, ignore this unmanned capability and the benefits it generates. Look at the last 20 years and the fantastic scientific advancements in unmanned technology that we've experienced. For example, the computer age has spread like wildfire, enabling enormous improvements in safety and risk mitigation by not sending a live pilot into enemy territory.

War Memories

When Ralph thought of WWII, the first thing that came to mind was the P-38. He was hung up on flying P-38s in WWII as he progressed through flight training. He even volunteered to go to twin-engine advanced training as that was the only way to fly the twin engine P-38. The instructors tried to talk him into staying at pilot training as an instructor and he always said, "Hell no, I'm not interested in coming back here. I want to fly in combat."[155]

He just loved the way the P-38 handled. He'd say, "That thing could turn inside its own ass." It had what

---

[154] (R. S. Parr, personal interview)

[155] (R. S. Parr, personal interview)

248

they called combat flaps. These flaps came down 30 degrees on the back side of the inner wing near the fuselage, providing an increased lift capability and thus, increasing the aircraft turn rate. You could drop those flaps in the turn, and it would literally suck the aircraft through a turn in a hurry. It was the best thing going, in its day.

Ralph's most visual recollection of Korea was the awesome countryside. It was beautiful but 'junglish'. His time spent on the ground as a FAC wasn't a very pleasant experience regarding the work aspect, but it was always very green and scenic.

He was offered an astronaut slot upon his return from Korea. He said, "In all honesty, I don't think so because I'll be gone from home all the time, and I owe it to my kids to spend some time at home after two tours in Korea." So, the air force offered him a Thunderbird slot, and although he was flattered at the shot to fly with the air force's flight demonstration team, he felt obligated to decline that position as well for the same reason.[156]

Ralph thoroughly enjoyed the flying in Vietnam, especially missions out of Cam Ranh Bay where he had a lot of great sorties and made some great friends while stationed there. He rarely saw General MacArthur during that assignment as whenever Ralph was tasked to attend the upper management meetings, MacArthur spent most of his time with the government agencies in downtown Tokyo, adjacent to the palace. The general was too engrossed in the strategies and tactics for upcoming campaigns and missions to have any spare time for visits.

---

[156] (R. S. Parr, personal interview)

Vietnam was a much-politicized war. Ralph found that the tacticians would define the targets, but the actual target lists were coming out of D.C. and that pissed the deployed pilots off. They felt that they were missing key opportunities in degrading the enemy's war-making capabilities by seeing targets (from the air) that 'needed' to be hit and then finding out those targets didn't make the approved target list out of D.C. the next day when they showed up to fly their sorties. He felt that the wrong people were calling the shots. But they had to abide by the orders out of Washington.[157]

He didn't recall much about Desert Storm because he'd been retired for nearly 16 years and he spent so many consecutive years in and out of the hospital with back surgeries and doctor visits to continue closely tracking all of the current military actions. He felt that the success of actions in Desert Storm was probably forged from lessons learned during Vietnam. The United States Government let Generals Schwarzkopf and Horner call the shots and make all the major wartime decisions in theatre with amazing results.

Losing My Kids—Worst Days of My Life

Ralph suffered from nightmares throughout the later years of his life. The doctors attempted to treat his nightmares for years through medication that kept him in a state of sleep, not allowing them to occur. He didn't know which war his nightmares took him back to, but he felt that they were from Korea and Vietnam. They

---

[157] (R. S. Parr, personal interview)

normally didn't have anything to do with airplanes or flying.

His most traumatic nightmares didn't come from fighting in a war; they came from losing his two wonderful kids. It is without a doubt a parent's worst nightmare.

He lost his daughter, Pamela, first in 2006, and then lost his son, Ralph S. III, in 2009. Each passed away from lung cancer. Ralph fought with the reasoning as to why he couldn't convince them to quit smoking. The more they smoked, the more they wanted to smoke, and anything he said, or thought didn't matter to either of them. Pamela was living in Nashville at the time. Ralph made three trips to Tennessee and had just returned from the third trip, and no sooner got home when doctors called to tell him that she had died. He was literally devastated.

His son went about the same way as he got pains in his chest and decided to go see the doctor. The doctor told him that he wasn't going to make it a week. He died two or three days later.

During Ralph's final year of life, he sat in his assisted living home in New Braunfels, TX, suffering from lung cancer that had spread to his liver and lymph nodes, and he never smoked a day in his life. *Sometimes, life's just not fair,* he thought.

He felt blessed to have been married to his second wife, Margaret, for more than 40 years. He met her at the Randolph Officer's Club (renamed the Parr O'Club in 2008). There's a great basement bar there called the Auger Inn, which Ralph frequented until he literally couldn't make the 30-minute trip from New Braunfels anymore. He lived each week for his Friday afternoons at the club. A mutual friend of him and Margaret's introduced them in late 1968 or 1969, and they hit it off right from the start. He said, "I wasn't sure if it was love at first sight, but she was a good lookin' lil muffin," with a grin on his face. They were married at the end of 1969. He always said that he would never publish how he proposed to her, but they were married at the Randolph AFB chapel. He went straight to Vietnam after their wedding as he was already on orders to go for his second tour, and thus departed for Phu Cat.

One of Ralph's fondest memories of more than 40 years that he spent with Margaret was when they met for a week-long vacation in Honolulu during the war. They had such a great time together.

Margaret had three children from a previous marriage: Paul, Linda, and Sheryl. Linda, being the youngest of the three, spent the most time with her mother and Ralph. He worked hard to treat each of the three of them as his own, and they reciprocated by treating him well and calling him Dad. Thank God for them, as they each were a true blessing for Ralph as he grew with age and were with him till the end.[158]

OFAS and Friendships

One night, 'Pick' (Col. Ed Pickrel, USAF (Ret.)) and Ralph were sitting at the bar in the Auger Inn, chatting about their time in Vietnam. After visiting for a while, they decided to go over to join a table where there were about a half-dozen guys sitting around, telling similar

---

[158] (R. S. Parr, personal interview)

war stories. They called themselves 'OFAS' or Old Farts Association. In the later years, that table became the Friday afternoon meeting place, where they could relax and trade war stories. On so many occasions, there would be young aviators, still in training, sitting there, soaking up those war stories like a sponge. The untested aviator trainees were trying to pick up tidbits of information that they could put in their memory banks for later use. It was hard to fathom who was enjoying the conversation more, the old guys reminiscing or the youngsters in their new nomex flightsuits intently listening to every word they spoke. Ralph said that it turned out to be their weekly hangar fly session, which he truly enjoyed because of their company. "They're all good guys," he said, "It was a great change of pace and healthy."

Many friendships he made in the military turned out to be lifelong friends. Guys like 'Boots' Blesse who was a helluva good pilot. They were peers and friendly competitors; Vermont Garrison, Lonny Moore, and Ralph came into the F-86 squadron at the same time; Tom McManus, Ralph's backseater in Vietnam, is a lifelong friend. Pancho Pasqualicchio flew P-51s with Ralph in the mid-1940s.

Devol 'Rock' Brett was at Cam Ranh Bay with Ralph and retired as a 3-star general. He was a helluva a good F-86 pilot. Robert J. Dixon was a retired 4-star and has passed away. John Roberts was great gunnery pilot and has since passed. James K. Johnson was a Korean War Ace and a great friend. Ralph would run out of daylight before he ran out of life-long friends to talk about.

Ralph felt that pilots like Jimmy Jabara and Al Cox made him a better man and pilot for knowing those guys.

Al was killed in 1953 when Ralph's other wingman crossed under the flight. He misjudged his maneuver and was tossed right into Al's aircraft when he hit Ralph's jet wash. Neither one of them was able to eject after the collision. The loss of those two pilots was very rough on the entire squadron. That's a prime example of flying being an inherently dangerous occupation. [159]

Jimmy Jabara was the first American jet ace and ended up being a triple ace with 15 MiG kills to his credit. 'Jabby' and his daughter were killed in a car accident in 1966. An airport on the outskirts of Wichita, Kansas, was named Colonel James Jabara Airport in his memory.

Should Have Died So Many Times

Ralph thought that he was a goner on numerous occasions. In Iran, Ralph's predecessor was targeted, and they were successful in attacking him. Being followed all the time pissed Ralph off, so he thought that he'd do a little detective work on his own. One day, he got the license plate number from the vehicle following him. He discovered that the license plates were issued depending on which part of town you lived. Once Ralph's security forces found the car and associated residence; they raided the outfit and a massive gunfight erupted. As a result, all of the terrorists in the house were killed that day.

Then one day out of nowhere, Ralph's executive officer was killed. Ralph had told him weekly, "Do not go out the front door until the staff car is at your house, waiting for you." His exec decided that it was a nice day,

---

[159] (R. S. Parr, personal interview)

so he stepped out early for a breath of fresh air during his walk down to the corner to catch his staff car for the ride into work. The staff car didn't arrive or was a little late that day. A terrorist stepped out from around the corner and shot him in the back of the head, instantly killing him.

Then there was that Chinese infantryman in Korea, who fired his sub-machine gun through the Jeep's windshield right between Ralph and his interpreter. Fortunately, he missed, only riddling the Jeep full of bullet holes. The vision of the Jeep's cockpit, which erupted like the largest fireworks display you can recall, was one Ralph would never forget.

The other time Ralph thought that he was a goner, and had actually accepted it, was when he was pulling out of the dive at Mach one. His F-86 was nearing terminal velocity as he jumped two flights of eight MiG-15s. At the time, he thought, *Shit, I'm not gonna make it.* It took both fists clenched around the top of the aircraft's stick and a double arm pull to reach 9.5 Gs, enabling him to pull out of the dive and leveling off at 300 feet above the ground. He was flying so fast that the air was building up on the front of his wings and vapor was forming as he rocketed straight toward the ground. The medal Ralph earned for that particular mission said that he bounced a flight of 10 MiGs. He'd never jumped a flight of 10 aircraft. There were 16 MiGs that day. Yes, he probably should have died on numerous occasions.[160]

IL-12 Shootdown Fallout

[160] (R. S. Parr, personal interview)

When he first came back from Korea, he couldn't leave the country without notifying a specific 'somebody'.[161] He could only fly on aircraft owned by the United States and he was required to gain permission to leave. He couldn't fly over any non-allied country for safety reasons. The importance of the people killed on his last aircraft shootdown, the IL-12, probably drove these actions. This wore hard on his psyche.[162]

When he landed on Iranian soil, he was an immediate target, marked for removal. He felt that a portion of his life could be part of why he suffered from nightmares, but he rarely remembered everything he dreamt. One dream reoccurred from time to time though. He knew what everybody was going to do, going to say, etc. It was surreal.

The Need to Belong

Everyone feels the need to belong. Ralph was no different, whether it is civic organizations, military organizations, or a group of people that you simply enjoy visiting with over a cup of coffee.

God knows he loved to fly when he was young. But later in life, Ralph satisfied his need to belong by attending the quarterly fighter ace luncheons held in San Antonio up until his passing. At one meeting, the president of the San Antonio organization voluntarily stood up and said that a recently deceased 4-star General

---

[161] When pressed on this question, Ralph would never divulge who in the government he must notify when he had plans to leave the country.

[162] (R. S. Parr, personal interview)

said (before his passing) that Ralph Parr was the best fighter pilot he'd ever known. General Dixon had been Ralph's wingman in Korea and Ralph was very humbled to hear those words spoken of him. Gen. Dixon retired as the commander of Tactical Air Command, now known as Air Combat Command.

Red River Valley Fighter Pilot Association

Ralph felt extremely honored to belong to the 'Ralph Parr Pack', the San Antonio Chapter of the Red River Valley Fighter Pilot Association. This national organization was founded by Colonel Robin Olds, the commander of the 8th Tactical Fighter Wing, when he hosted a Tactics Conference at Ubon AFB, Thailand, in November 1966. It included United States Air Force, Navy, and Marine aircrews that were flying combat missions over the 'Red River Valley of North Vietnam'. In May 1967, the 388th Tactical Fighter Wing at Korat, KTAFB, Thailand, held the first of five practice reunions in Thailand. Others were held at Ubon in August 1967, Takhli in November 1967, Udorn in March 1968, and Korat in June 1968.

In 1969, Brigadier General Robin Olds met with Colonel Scrappy Johnson to discuss the formation of a permanent association for the Red River Valley Fighter Pilots Association. The association was subsequently incorporated. In 1969, Col. Larry Pickett held the first stateside practice reunion at Wichita, Kansas and it was a great success.

The organization, its purposes, and efforts were directed toward generating awareness of the Prisoners of

War (POW), as well as aircrews Missing in Action/Killed in Action (MIA/KIA) and their families.

The scholarship program is a major priority of this organization. The fund was established at the San Antonio reunion in 1970 as a result of concern for the families of fellow 'River Rats' who were POW/MIA/KIA. The hat was passed, and three $1,000 scholarships were awarded.

In August 1973, after the prisoners of war had returned home, the first 'real' reunion was held in Las Vegas, Nevada.

On April 30, 1975, the name was amended to 'Red River Valley Association, Inc.' On July 22, 1976, the 501(c) (3) status was granted by the IRS.

In 1998, the scholarship program was expanded to include losses due to non-combat operational accidents. The association now provides scholarships to children of United States military personnel MIA/KIA in armed conflict from Southeast Asia through the present. Additionally, dependents of aircrew members killed in aircraft accidents now qualify for scholarships.

Since 1970, 'The Red River Rats' have awarded more than 1,090 scholarship grants with a value of over $1.9 million. The Red River Valley Association continues to have reunions and award scholarships annually.

Giving back is something each of us should carry throughout our lives. The Red River Rats afforded Ralph the opportunity to do just that and to have the San Antonio Chapter named after him was a huge honor.

Ralph was also an active member of the AMVETS, Daedalians, VFW, and Air Force Association.

Re-attacks?

There's nothing that Ralph wished he could do over again. Would he make any changes? He thought about it once in a while, but nothing specific ever came to mind. He always wanted to maintain his goal of treating others as he'd want to be treated.

Remembered

Ralph wanted to be remembered for a couple of things: 1) that he knew how to fly an airplane well, and 2) he always tried to be fair to his people.

He was always known as a fix-it guy. If an outfit had problems, leadership seemed to always call on Ralph to go fix the problems or issues that it was experiencing. In a very short period of time, he progressed from being a captain in a flying squadron to an adjutant of a group, to the director of operations of a group, to the commander of the group. He was delighted in how his career progressed and the enjoyment that he received from the constant increased responsibilities.

Words for Troops

If you like what you're doing, you're gonna do well and you're gonna feel good about it. You'll be successful and productive. If you don't like what you're doing, you'll be miserable and detest your work. He was fortunate to hold fantastic jobs throughout his career.

Before Ralph passed away, he said that he wished he could tell the troops returning from Iraq and Afghanistan, 'Welcome home!' He'd give them a firm handshake and perhaps even a hug. There is no room for and no reason for anyone to scream, 'War monger!' to our returning troops. They were sent to carry out the government's orders and they are simply thankful and proud to be returning home to their families, alive.

National Anthem

Ralph's thought on the national anthem was a sore subject. He detested hearing performers personalize the national anthem. He thought that the national anthem ought to be sung out of respect and its tune or lyrics shouldn't be messed with.

Did he enjoy hearing it? Yes, he loved hearing it. He got extremely passionate when he'd say, "This is my country." If he could, he would have taken every American abroad for six months to visit various countries where he'd been stationed. Then, after those six months, let them come back to the good ole U.S.A. to see exactly what we've got here. Then, when they'd hear the national anthem, they'd get goose bumps, just like him, every time they hear it.

Americans, in general, take our lifestyle for granted. They think that everything is owed to them. Well, it was earned and at a very high price. There are many people responsible for getting our great nation to this point.

Returning from Vietnam

When Ralph came back from Vietnam, it was in the dark of the night as he walked down the gang plank of the ship in a San Francisco port. It was about 10 p.m. There were three or four hippies standing in his desired path. Ralph, in uniform, was spat at as he walked past. It really pissed him off. There was an MP nearby who hurried over and clubbed them with his night stick. Ralph thought, *Well, at least that will keep him from doing something more.*

He'd spent a lot of time overseas in deep shit up to that point, and being spat at was not what he expected upon his return, but they felt that it was their right. Ralph shrugged it off and thought, *Oh, well, what the hell. The sun is going to come up in the east tomorrow, and there's really nothing I can do about it.*

Goals and Short String

There are goals that he still wanted to achieve but he knew deep in his heart that he just couldn't get there from here. There was simply too much to do and not enough time to get it done. The thing that surprised him most was that so many people are afraid of dying, and that rattled his gourd because he didn't feel that way at all. "You live your life by the code that fits your life," he said. He found himself not wanting to waste much time as his days dwindled.

About one month before Ralph passed away, he said the following in a heartfelt interview: "The talk of me, one day, earning the Medal of Honor for the mission at Khe Sanh is extremely humbling. That's not why I was in the fight, to win a medal. The heroism, valor, and earned medals are results of what every one of us was doing on a daily basis while at war. Our willingness to accept the risks of that next mission were driven by patriotism and the fire in our hearts to defend the ideals of this great nation. At least, my family knows that the reason I fought the fight was to defend the constitution and preserve the freedoms, values, and principles our forefathers drafted well over 200 years ago. They'll know that I had the interest of all future generations in my heart and carried that to my grave."[163]

Gen. Douglas MacArthur once said, "Old soldiers never die; they just fade away."

Ralph was an old soldier; he relished that fact. Everyone is issued a certain length of string when they're born and as his string neared its end, it was time to tell his story. Should this story persuade one person to strive for an improved or newly refined vector in life, then it's served its purpose.

Ralph's string has reached its end and he's currently on a flight never to land. Now, it's time to rest.

Colonel Ralph S. Parr died on 7 December 2012 in New Braunfels, TX from complications of cancer. Ironically, his passing was on the anniversary date of the Japanese bombing of Pearl Harbor, a day that sparked his entry into the United States Army Air Corps and America's entry into WWII. He was laid to rest at the Fort Sam Houston National Cemetery in San Antonio, Texas ten days later.

---

[163] (R. S. Parr, personal interview)

A flight of T-38 Talons from the 560th Flying Training Squadron at Randolph AFB performs a missing man formation fly by at Colonel Parr's interment ceremony at Fort Sam Houston's National Cemetery in San Antonio, TX.

Chapter 16
"What Others Say . . ."

"Ralph Parr is an American Hero!"

By Maj. Gen. Jacqueline Van Ovost, USAF

"It was early in 2008 that I first met Col. Ralph Parr. It was brought to my attention that this Korean War Double Ace was still actively mentoring our newest aviators at Randolph AFB, Texas, the home of Airpower's Blacksmiths."

Every Friday night, you could find Ralph at the 'Auger Inn,' the basement of the famous Randolph AFB Officer's Club. There, he would be describing, to a very attentive audience of young aviators, each detail of air battles long past. The young and old would press in close to hear about his first tour in Korea, and then going back a second time with the new F-86 Sabre jet fighter. The Vietnam flying action also was played out as these youngsters had just read books on the tactics that he had developed. Now, they had a face-to-face interaction with a real aviator hero, who flew in some of the biggest adventures to be had in those times.

Col. Parr mentors three young aviators during his 88th birthday party held at the Auger Inn in July 2012.

Col. Richard Clark, then commander of Randolph AFB, invited Col. Parr to be a guest speaker at our Combat Dining In. As you can imagine, 'combat' play was a bit aggressive, and we were somewhat concerned about his safety at the head of the table. Our security forces team literally shielded him with riot shields until the combat play was over. He would proceed to tell our airmen and civilians about his last few weeks in Korea when he became a double ace. It was truly amazing to see these warriors, all wet and somewhat scuffed by the horseplay, gather and sit around Col. Parr, hanging on his every word. He spoke softly, and they were straining to hear his account of that heroic day. He was captivating!

Col. Ralph Parr is not just any ace aviator and Air Force Cross recipient gracing the home of Air Education and Training Command's premier pilot instructor base. As a former commander of the 12th Tactical Fighter Wing, 1970-1971, Col. Parr is a part of our lineage in the

12th Flying Training Wing. His picture is proudly displayed among previous commanders in the headquarters building, the 'Taj Mahal.' He would often stop by to visit 12th FTW commanders to mentor us with feedback on the wing performance or provide a relevant story for the time. Once, word got out that Col. Parr was in the building; airmen would flock to see him in the office.

At the time, we were looking for someone to name our Officer's Club after to further air force legacy and tradition. We didn't have far to look. This legendary hero was right in our midst and still very much a part of grooming young aviators. On December 5, 2008, Col. Parr's legend was immortalized by renaming the Randolph Officer's Club the 'Parr O'Club.' It was my honor to perform the simple, but momentous, ceremony on behalf of our air force. He is certainly a shining example of an airman who has contributed greatly beyond his 34-year military career.

As famous and illustrious as Col. Parr is in life, he is still one of our most humble servants. He will only come forward with the stories when asked, and even then, only quietly. With each visit to the Parr O'Club and the Auger Inn, he shared a part of himself, his warrior spirit. He asked nothing in return except for blue skies and safety for each of our aviators. He was such a treasure to this country. He was truly a large part of the 'Greatest Generation' who molded this country's finest military."

Ralph Parr, A Stick and Rudder Artist

By Robert 'Pancho' Pasqualicchio

As WWII drew to a close, there was massive downsizing. Many guys exited the army air corps to attend college. In our case, it was a chance to form a bond and our version of the three musketeers. Ralph Parr, Bill Hall, and I were all going to college in near Washington, D.C., at the time. We started flying P-51s in the reserves out of Andrews Field in 1946. When the reserves lost their airplanes due to budget constraints, we decided that we'd go over to the Air National Guard to fly P-47s with them in 1947. We earned a few bucks for a day's pay while flying P-47s. That would help us with our $55-per-month college budget. We were so hungry to fly in those days that one day, we went to the Chinese Embassy in D.C. to see if Chiang Kai-shek wanted to start another Flying Tigers Squadron... We would have rather flown than eat. After flying together for a year or so, the three of us decided that we wanted to get back into the army air corps.

We generated all the required paperwork and took our packages over to the Pentagon. There was a women's army corps (WAC) gal who worked in the office and accepted our applications. Her inbox had a stack of 'return to active duty' packages that was about four-inches deep. We came out of her office and I said, "Guys, one of us has to make the supreme sacrifice and romance that gal if we want to have a snowball's chance in hell of getting our packages through that office. We're gonna draw straws, and the guy who draws the short straw has to go out and romance that gal."

She wasn't very good looking. The two longer straws had to each pay $20 to finance the romance. Well, Bill Hall drew the short straw, so Ralph and I chipped in the $40 finance fee, and Hall's courtship with the WAC resulted in us flying P-51s in Roswell, New Mexico, within two months. Bill Hall has since passed away, but Ralph and I still get a laugh out of that story.

After flying P-51s, we went to F-84C models. Performance issues wouldn't let us take off after 10:00 a.m. local time due to high temperatures and pressure altitude. So, the fighter group was moved to Otis Field on Cape Cod. The three of us were assigned to different squadrons and eventually split up to the four winds in 1948. I went to Panama, Ralph went to Korea, and Bill went to fly SAC fighters and eventually U-2s.

We bummed together and lived together in those days, and the thing I remember most about Ralph was that he had the eyes of a hawk and could fly any aircraft with a beautiful touch. He was a fantastic aviator. There's proof in the pudding. We stayed in touch for the next 70 years and remained great buddies until he passed away. I've flown with Chuck Yeager and other guys of similar caliber, and Ralph ranks right up there with the best.

A natural aviator is always prepared and ready to go on any mission. Ralph had the talent to fly and could put the machine in any piece of airspace he wanted. He knew what he needed to do to be successful. He was just a sweetheart of a pilot. Young fighter pilots who want to emulate a hero should emulate Ralph Parr's manor of behavior and his drive to gain knowledge of every airplane that he flew. He was a true stick and rudder artist.

A Historic Man

By JF 'Nails' Knight, Lt. Col., USAF (Ret.)

By the time I first flew in the same aircraft with Col. Ralph Parr, I had completed a tour in Vietnam and accumulated 2,000 hours flying time in three different USAF fighter aircraft. I was fortunate to fly with him several times, as he upgraded me to instructor pilot in the F-4 Phantom. Since that time, I flew with many others as an instructor in a Replacement Training Unit or RTU. The experience gives me the confidence to make a judgment on the gifts of the man. I do realize that by the time I flew with him, due to the inroads of father time, some of those gifts might not have been quite as sharp as they had been, but those that remained were awe-inspiring.

One of his most remarkable attributes was his vision. He saw things that were beyond the visual range of the average pilot. Equally important was his extraordinary feel and handling of the aircraft, which approached the incredible. Combine this with his remarkable record of accomplishments in three wars, and the result is one of the most dedicated, decorated, and famous names in aviation history.

It is my privilege to have known the man.

APPENDIX I
Awards and Citations

Air Force Cross
Awarded for actions during the Vietnam War

The President of the United States of America, authorized by Title 10, Section 8742, United States Code, takes pleasure in presenting the Air Force Cross to Colonel Ralph Sherman Parr (AFSN: 0-28206), United States Air Force, for extraordinary heroism in military operations against an opposing force as an F-4C Aircraft Commander and Commanding officer of the 12th Tactical Fighter Wing, Cam Ranh Bay Air Base, Vietnam, in action near Khe Sanh, Republic of Vietnam, on 16 March 1968.

On that date, Colonel Parr participated in a flight, providing cover for cargo aircraft. Upon arrival over the target, the forward air controller advised the flight that the airfield was under heavy attack by hostile mortar positions, which were located a few feet below a ridge line. Although the target area was covered with dense smoke and haze, Colonel Parr successfully destroyed one mortar position on his first pass, as six well-camouflaged heavy automatic weapons opened fire on him. Although sustaining severe damage to his aircraft, he pressed his second attack and destroyed another mortar position.

Again, completely disregarding his personal safety and the withering hostile gun fire, Colonel Parr succeeded in destroying six heavy caliber automatic weapons positions. In between passes, his accurate and timely directions to his wingman effectively insured the accuracy of ordnance delivery in close proximity to the friendly forces. Only after delivering all of his ordnance at point-blank range in eight consecutive passes did Colonel Parr terminate his attack.

By destroying these strategically located weapons, he not only impaired the hostile force's capability to impede the resupply of Khe Sanh but also reduced further losses to friendly cargo aircraft and crews. Through his superb airmanship, aggressiveness, and extraordinary heroism, Colonel Parr reflected the highest credit upon himself and the United States Air Force.

Action Date: 16-Mar-1968
Service: Air Force
Rank: Colonel
Company: Commanding Officer
Regiment: 12th Tactical Fighter Wing
Division: Cam Ranh Bay Air Base, Vietnam

Distinguished Service Cross
Awarded for actions during the Korean War

The President of the United States of America, under the provisions of the Act of Congress approved 9 July 1918, takes pleasure in presenting the Distinguished Service Cross to Captain Ralph Sherman Parr (AFSN: 0-28206), United States Air Force, for extraordinary heroism in connection with military operations against an armed enemy of the United Nations while serving as pilot of an F-86 type aircraft of the 334th Fighter-Interceptor Squadron, 4th Fighter-Interceptor Wing, FIFTH Air Force, in action against enemy forces in the Republic of Korea on 30 June 1953.

On that date, while leading a formation of two F-86 type aircraft on a combat air patrol deep in enemy territory, Captain Parr was attacked by a formation of ten enemy MIGs. Exhibiting superb airmanship and extraordinary gallantry, Captain Parr positioned himself on the attackers. Despite the imminent threat from the hail of cannon fire from behind, Captain Parr selected his target, and with a long burst from his guns, destroyed one of the enemy MIGs. Against superior numbers of enemy aircraft, Captain Parr, although under a continual hail of enemy cannon fire and with complete disregard for his personal safety, again valiantly counter-attacked another of the threatening aircraft.

Utilizing extraordinary flying skill, Captain Parr tenaciously followed the enemy through a series of violent, evasive maneuvers until he gained the advantage and scored multiple hits on the MiG, causing it to burst into flames. While turning to move to surprise another of the enemy aircraft, Captain Parr broke off his attack to answer a call of distress from a friendly aircraft.

Although dangerously low on fuel, Captain Parr, at great risk to his life, provided aggressive and determined protection for the distressed friendly aircraft, escorting it safely back to the base. Captain Parr's keen flying skill in turning the tide of battle despite overwhelming odds and his high personal courage in protecting a fellow pilot evidenced conspicuous gallantry in action and reflected great credit upon himself, the Far East Air Forces and the United States Air Force.

General Orders: Headquarters, Far East Air Forces: General Orders No. 33 (27 February 1954)
Action Date: 30-Jun-1953
Service: Air Force
Rank: Captain
Company: 334th Fighter-Interceptor Squadron
Regiment: 4th Fighter-Interceptor Wing
Division: 5th Air Force

Silver Star
Awarded for actions during the Korean War

The President of the United States of America, authorized by Act of Congress 9 July 1918, takes pleasure in presenting the Silver Star to Captain Ralph Sherman Parr (AFSN: 0-28206), United States Air Force, for conspicuous gallantry and intrepidity in action against an enemy of the United Nations as pilot of an F-86 aircraft, 4th Fighter-Interceptor Wing, FIFTH Air Force, in action on 18 June 1953 in Korea.

On that date, while leading a formation of two F-86s on a combat patrol deep in enemy territory near the Yalu River, Captain Parr sighted three enemy aircraft and immediately initiated a vertical-diving attack. In executing the violent maneuvers for the attack, Captain Parr and his wingman became separated. Although outnumbered three-to-one, Captain Parr gallantly continued his attack, focusing his action on one of the MiGs. By skillfully maneuvering, Captain Parr raked his target with accurate fire along the fuselage, causing the MiG to crash and explode. He immediately turned to face the threat of the other two enemy MiGs and became involved in a desperate dogfight.

In the ensuing action, Captain Parr fired a concentrated burst which ripped a wing completely off one of the MiGs, causing the enemy aircraft to disintegrate and the remaining MiG to flee across the Yalu River. Through this demonstration of superb airmanship, high courage and gallantry in the face of a determined enemy, Captain Parr reflected great credit upon himself, the Far East Air Forces and the United States Air Force.

Action Date: 18-Jun-1953
Service: Air Force
Rank: Captain
Company: 334th Fighter-Interceptor Squadron
Regiment: 4th Fighter-Interceptor Wing
Division: 5th Air Force

Legion of Merit
Awarded for actions during the Vietnam War

The President of the United States of America, authorized by Act of Congress, 20 July 1942, takes pleasure in presenting the Legion of Merit to Colonel Ralph Sherman Parr (AFSN: 0-28206), United States Air Force, for exceptionally meritorious conduct in the performance of outstanding services to the Government of the United States as vice commander and commander, 12th Tactical Fighter Wing, MacDill Air Base, Republic of Vietnam from 11 March 1970 to 20 February 1971.

In these positions of critical responsibility, the executive leadership, capable planning, and strength of purpose demonstrated by Colonel Parr resulted in significant achievements and improvements in the employment of tactical air power in combat. His superior management of combat resources, sound judgment, and his vast knowledge of military tactics were of immeasurable value to the successful accomplishment of the United States mission in Southeast Asia. The superior initiative, outstanding leadership, and personal endeavor displayed by Colonel Parr reflect great credit upon himself and the United States Air Force.

Action Date: 11 March 1970 – 20 February 1971
Service: Air Force
Rank: Colonel

Legion of Merit

The President of the United States of America, authorized by Act of Congress, 2 July 1926, takes pleasure in presenting a Bronze Oak Leaf Cluster in lieu of a Second Award of the Legion of Merit to Colonel Ralph Sherman Parr (AFSN: 0-28206), United States Air Force, for exceptionally meritorious conduct in the performance of outstanding services to the Government of the United States as chief of staff, Headquarters United States Military Mission with the Iranian Army and United States Military Assistance Advisory Group to Iran, from 29 August 1972 to 3 January 1974.

Colonel Parr's actions on many sensitive projects made significant contributions to the United States national policy relating to matters in the Middle East. He singularly made outstanding contributions to increase the interface of the United States Mission in Iran to such an extent that our diplomatic and military relations with that country have materialized as a stabilizing influence in the volatile Middle East environment. The singularly distinctive accomplishments of Colonel Parr reflect great credit upon himself and the United States Air Force.

Action Date: 29 August 1972 – 3 January 1974

Service: Air Force
Rank: Colonel

Legion of Merit

The President of the United States of America, authorized by Act of Congress, 2 July 1926, takes pleasure in presenting a Second Bronze Oak Leaf Cluster in lieu of a Third Award of the Legion of Merit to Colonel Ralph Sherman Parr (AFSN: 0-28206), United States Air Force, for exceptionally meritorious conduct in the performance of outstanding services to the Government of the United States as Director of Operations, United States Air Force Tactical Air Warfare Center, Tactical Air Command, and as Chief of Staff, Armament Development and Test Center, Air Force Systems Command, Eglin Air Force Base, Florida, from 30 January 1974 to 15 August 1976.

With extraordinary professionalism and personal dedication, Colonel Parr applied the highest standards of executive management in both highlighting and solving problems involving center efforts of national importance. His personal ability, diligence, and devotion to duty contributed immeasurably to the successful accomplishment of the air force mission. The singularly distinctive accomplishments of Colonel Parr culminate a long and distinguished career in the service of his country and reflect great credit upon himself and the United States Air Force.

Action Date: 30 January 1974 – 15 August 1976
Service: Air Force
Rank: Colonel

Distinguished Flying Cross
Awarded for actions during the World War II

(Citation Needed) - SYNOPSIS: Captain Ralph Sherman Parr (AFSN: 0-28206), United States Air Force, was awarded the Distinguished Flying Cross for extraordinary achievement while participating in aerial flight.

Action Date: World War II
Service: Air Force
Rank: Captain
Company: 334th Fighter-Interceptor Squadron
Regiment: 4th Fighter-Interceptor Wing
Division: 5th Air Force

Distinguished Flying Cross
Awarded for actions during the Korean War

The President of the United States of America, authorized by Act of Congress, 2 July 1926, takes pleasure in presenting a Bronze Oak Leaf Cluster in lieu of a Second Award of the Distinguished Flying Cross to Captain Ralph Sherman Parr (AFSN: 0-28206), United States Air Force, for extraordinary achievement while participating in aerial flight on 10 June 1953, in aerial combat against enemies of the United Nations in Korea, as pilot of an F-86 aircraft, 4th Fighter Interceptor Wing, FIFTH Air Force.

On this day, Captain Parr was flying in a flight of four F-86s on a patrol deep within North Korea. As they neared the Yalu River, Captain Parr's flight was attacked by a large force of MiGs and split up into elements of two, but he and his wingman evaded the MiGs in the break.

Captain Parr then observed two more MiGs heading for the Yalu River, using clouds for concealment. He and his wingman headed for them in a high-speed dive. Captain Parr broke out of the clouds on the MiGs at a very close range, and although he was having trouble controlling his aircraft due to the high speed, he nevertheless opened fire, placing a concentrated burst of fire into the MiG's engine section. The MiG was observed to explode.

Although Captain Parr's aircraft sustained damage from parts of the enemy aircraft flying back, he was able to control his aircraft, and upon returning safely to his home base, was credited with the destruction of one MiG-15. This action is typical of the outstanding courage and exceptionally aggressive flying ability of Captain Parr and reflects great credit upon himself and the United States Air Force.

Action Date: 10-Jun-1953
Service: Air Force
Rank: Captain
Regiment: 4th Fighter-Interceptor Wing
Division: 5th Air Force

Distinguished Flying Cross
Awarded for actions during the Korean War

The President of the United States of America, authorized by Act of Congress, 2 July 1926, takes pleasure in presenting a Second Bronze Oak Leaf Cluster in lieu of a Third Award of the Distinguished Flying Cross to Captain Ralph Sherman Parr (AFSN: 0-28206), United States Air Force, for extraordinary achievement while participating in aerial flight on 19 June 1953, in aerial combat against enemies of the United Nations in Korea, as pilot of an F-86 aircraft, 4th Fighter Interceptor Wing, FIFTH Air Force.

On this date, Captain Parr was leading a flight of four F-86s, flying protective cover for a slow flying reconnaissance aircraft when the RF-80 was attacked by an enemy MiG-15. As the MiG pulled up to fire on the unarmed RF-80, Captain Parr attacked the enemy MiG, and closing to 1,500 feet, fired a long burst directly into the MiG's fuselage. The MiG immediately caught fire, and just before it spun into the ground and crashed, the pilot was observed to eject.

At this time, another MiG-15 attacked the reconnaissance aircraft, and Captain Parr again initiated another vicious attack. He closed to 1,800-feet range and fired several bursts at the enemy aircraft, scoring multiple hits and causing the enemy to break off the attack on the RF-80.

Captain Parr then escorted the reconnaissance aircraft to his remaining targets and back to friendly territory safely. Upon return to his home base, Captain Parr was officially credited with destroying one MiG-15 and damaging another. This action is another example of the outstanding flying ability and fearless courage of Captain Parr and reflects great credit upon himself and the United States Air Force.

Action Date: 19-Jun-1953
Service: Air Force
Rank: Captain
Company: 334th Fighter-Interceptor Squadron
Regiment: 4th Fighter-Interceptor Wing
Division: 5th Air Force

Distinguished Flying Cross
Awarded for actions during the Korean War

The President of the United States of America, authorized by Act of Congress, 2 July 1926, takes pleasure in presenting a Third Bronze Oak Leaf Cluster in lieu of a Fourth Award of the Distinguished Flying Cross to Captain Ralph Sherman Parr (AFSN: 0-28206), United States Air Force, for extraordinary achievement while participating in aerial combat against the enemies of the United Nations in Korea, on 7 June 1953, as pilot of an F-86 aircraft, 4th Fighter Interceptor Wing, 5th Air Force.

On this day, Captain Parr was flying number-four man in a four-ship flight deep within enemy-held territory when he sighted two enemy MiGs far below his flight. Captain Parr saw that he was the only aircraft in the flight that had a tactical advantage on the enemy aircraft and received permission from his element leader to attack the MiGs. Captain Parr rolled over into a vicious diving attack and began firing on the MiGs.

During the battle, Captain Parr's gunsight ceased to function, but without the gunsight, Captain Parr still managed to destroy one of the MiGs and damage the other MiG. Captain Parr was then attacked by six more MiGs who had observed the battle. Captain Parr broke hard to the left as the lead MiG of the attacking force opened fire on him and began a series of violent maneuvers to elude the attacking MiGs. The lead MiG tried to turn inside of Captain Parr on the initial break and in doing so, lost control of his aircraft and was seen to snap and enter a spin near the ground. The MiG pilot ejected just before his aircraft hit the ground and exploded.

Captain Parr was credited with the destruction of two MiGs and the damage of one MiG on this mission. This action is an example of the outstanding courage and exceptional flying and tactical abilities of Captain Parr, which brought great credit upon himself, the United Nations and the United States Air Force.

Action Date: 7-Jun-1953
Service: Air Force
Rank: Captain
Company: 334th Fighter-Interceptor Squadron
Regiment: 4th Fighter-Interceptor Wing
Division: 5th Air Force

Distinguished Flying Cross
Awarded for actions during the Korean War

The President of the United States of America, authorized by Act of Congress, 2 July 1926, takes pleasure in presenting a Fourth Bronze Oak Leaf Cluster in lieu of a Fifth Award of the Distinguished Flying Cross to Captain Ralph Sherman Parr (AFSN: 0-28206), United States Air Force, for extraordinary achievement while participating in aerial flight on 12 July 1953 in aerial combat against an enemy of the United Nations in Korea while piloting an F-86 aircraft of the 4th Fighter Interceptor Wing, FIFTH Air Force.

While leading a two-ship flight of F-86s on a combat air patrol in North Korea, Captain Parr sighted a formation of four enemy MiG-15s crossing the Yalu to the South, using a low cloud cover for concealment. Immediately initiating a high-speed diving maneuver, Captain Parr dived through the overcast to attack, as he closed to fire, two of the enemy aircraft evaded him by crossing the Yalu.

The two remaining enemy MiGs turned hard into Captain Parr's attack, but through superior skill, he maneuvered his aircraft into attacking position and brought his guns to bear on one of the MiGs, scoring multiple hits in the engine section with several bursts of his deadly fire. The MiG began burning fiercely and desperately tried to escape, but Captain Parr tenaciously pursued the MiG, firing all the while. After scoring more hits on the enemy aircraft, the pilot was observed to eject and his flaming aircraft crashed into the ground.

Upon return to his home base, Captain Parr was officially credited with the destruction of one MiG-15. This action exemplifies the courage, superior skill, and aggressive airmanship displayed by Captain Parr throughout his combat tour and reflect great credit upon himself and the United States Air Force.

Action Date: 12-Jul-1953
Service: Air Force
Rank: Captain
Company: 334th Fighter-Interceptor Squadron
Regiment: 4th Fighter-Interceptor Wing
Division: 5th Air Force

Distinguished Flying Cross
Awarded for actions during the Vietnam War

The President of the United States of America, authorized by Act of Congress, 2 July 1926, takes pleasure in presenting a Silver Oak Leaf Cluster in lieu of a Sixth Award of the Distinguished Flying Cross to Colonel Ralph Sherman Parr (AFSN: 0-28206), United States Air Force, for extraordinary achievement while participating in aerial flight as an F-4C Aircraft Commander in Southeast Asia on 14 November 1967.

On that date, Colonel Parr led a mission over South Vietnam, against hostile ground forces engaged in combat with United States Army personnel in an outnumbered balance of troops. With complete disregard for his own personal safety, operating under marginal weather conditions and in the face of intense ground fire, Colonel Parr made multiple passes, inflicting major damage. The professional competence, aerial skill, and devotion to duty displayed by Colonel Parr reflect great credit upon himself and the United States Air Force.

General Orders: Headquarters, 7th Air Force, Special Orders No. G-1423 (15 May 1968)
Action Date: 14-Nov-1967

Service: Air Force
Rank: Colonel

Distinguished Flying Cross
Awarded for actions during the Vietnam War

The President of the United States of America, authorized by Act of Congress, 2 July 1926, takes pleasure in presenting a Bronze Oak Leaf Cluster in addition to a previously awarded Silver Oak Leaf Cluster in lieu of a Seventh Award of the Distinguished Flying Cross to Colonel Ralph Sherman Parr (AFSN: 0-28206), United States Air Force, for heroism in connection with military operations against an opposing armed force as an F-4C Aircraft Commander in Southeast Asia on 6 November 1967.

On that date, Colonel Parr led a mission in close support of friendly forces, struggling to defend the Dak To Special Forces Camp. Under intense hostile automatic weapons fire, Colonel Parr made multiple passes, delivering his ordnance with such devastating accuracy that the hostile elements were forced to make an unorganized withdrawal, leaving much of their equipment behind. The outstanding heroism and selfless devotion to duty displayed by Colonel Parr reflect great credit upon himself and the United States Air Force.

General Orders: Headquarters, 7th Air Force, Special Orders No. G-2035 (9 July 1968)
Action Date: 6-Nov-1967
Service: Air Force
Rank: Colonel

Distinguished Flying Cross
Awarded for actions during the Vietnam War

The President of the United States of America, authorized by Act of Congress, 2 July 1926, takes pleasure in presenting a Second Bronze Oak Leaf Cluster in addition to a previously awarded Silver Oak Leaf Cluster in lieu of an Eighth Award of the Distinguished Flying Cross to Colonel Ralph Sherman Parr (AFSN: 0-28206), United States Air Force, for extraordinary achievement while participating in aerial flight as an F-4C Aircraft Commander near Chu Lai, Republic of Vietnam on 5 June 1968.

On that date, Colonel Parr led a flight of fighters in support of friendly forces engaged with hostile forces under extremely difficult and hazardous weather conditions. Braving heavy ground fire, Colonel Parr delivered his ordnance with devastating accuracy and relieved the hostile pressure of the friendly forces. The professional competence, aerial skill, and devotion to duty displayed by Colonel Parr reflect great credit upon himself and the United States Air Force.

General Orders: Headquarters, 7th Air Force, Special Orders No. G-2661 (27 August 1968)

Action Date: 5-Jun-1968
Service: Air Force
Rank: Colonel

Distinguished Flying Cross
Awarded for actions during the Vietnam War

The President of the United States of America, authorized by Act of Congress, 2 July 1926, takes pleasure in presenting a Third Bronze Oak Leaf Cluster in addition to a previously awarded Silver Oak Leaf Cluster in lieu of a Ninth Award of the Distinguished Flying Cross to Colonel Ralph Sherman Parr (AFSN: 0-28206), United States Air Force, for heroism while participating in aerial flight as an aircraft commander near Dak To, Republic of Vietnam, on 13 April 1970.

On that date, Colonel Parr led a flight of two F-4Ds on an aerial strike mission in support of the besieged special forces who had been virtually overrun by a hostile force in excess of battalion strength. Despite the continuous barrage of hostile anti-aircraft, automatic weapons, and small arms fire, and with complete disregard for his personal safety, Colonel Parr attacked the well-entrenched hostile forces, making multiple passes and delivering at point-blank range to assure target destruction and avoid the friendly positions.

As a direct result of Colonel Parr's actions, the hostile force was annihilated and the stronghold was recaptured by the friendly forces, only hours after this air strike. The outstanding heroism and selfless devotion to duty displayed by Colonel Parr reflect great credit upon himself and the United States Air Force.

General Orders: Headquarters, 7th Air Force, Special Orders No. G-3239 (17 July 1970)
Action Date: 13-Apr-1970
Service: Air Force
Rank: Colonel

Distinguished Flying Cross
Awarded for actions during the Vietnam War

The President of the United States of America, authorized by Act of Congress, 2 July 1926, takes pleasure in presenting a Fourth Bronze Oak Leaf Cluster in addition to a previously awarded Silver Oak Leaf Cluster in lieu of a Tenth Award of the Distinguished Flying Cross to Colonel Ralph Sherman Parr (AFSN: 0-28206), United States Air Force, for extraordinary achievement while participating in aerial flight as an F-4D Aircraft Commander near Pleiku Air Base, Republic of Vietnam, on 18 May 1970.

On that date, Colonel Parr led a flight of two fighter aircraft in attacking an extremely dangerous hostile location. His expert tactical planning and extremely accurate ordnance delivery inflicted ten casualties on the hostile force and destroyed twenty-five military structures. The professional competence, aerial skill, and devotion to duty displayed by Colonel Parr reflect great credit upon himself and the United States Air Force.

Action Date: 18-May-1970
Service: Air Force

Rank: Colonel

APPENDIX II
Education and Service

Education:

High School: Bethesda-Chevy Chase H.S., Bethesda, MD, 1942

Military Basic Training, 1943

Flying Training: Pre-flight through Advanced, 1943 – Feb. 1944

American University, Washington, D.C., 1947

University of Arizona, Extension Course, 1955

University of Tampa, Extension Course, 1963-64

Air War College, Montgomery, AL, 1967

Service:

Nov. 1942 – Feb. 1944: Enlisted and Aviation Cadet

Feb. 1944 – Sept. 1944: Advanced Flying School Instructor

Oct. 1944 – June 1945: P-38 Fighter Training School

July 1945 – Sept. 1946: Pilot, Assistant Squadron Operations Officer, 49th Fighter Group (Philippines, Okinawa, and Japan)

49th Fighter Group

Feb. 1948 – June 1950: Flight Commander, 33rd Fighter Wing (Roswell AFB, NM, and Cape Cod, MA)

June 1950 – Apr. 1951: Squadron Flight Commander, 49th Fighter Wing (Taegu Air Base, South Korea)

49th Fighter Wing

7th Fighter Squadron

June 1951 – May 1953: Pilot, 94th Fighter-Interceptor Squadron (George AFB, CA)

94th Fighter-Interceptor Squadron

May 1953 – Jan. 1954: Pilot, Flight Commander, Squadron Operations Officer, 4th Fighter-Interceptor Wing (Kimpo Air Base, Korea)

4th Fighter-Interceptor Wing

Feb. 1954 – July 1958: Group Adjutant, Group Executive Officer, Wing Director of Operations, Air Defense Command Weapons Center (Yuma, AZ)

Aug. 1958 – Sept. 1959: Division Staff Operations Officer – 73rd Air Division (Tyndall AFB, FL)

73rd Air Division

Oct. 1959 – Sept. 1962: Staff Operations Officer, Military Assistance Group (MAAG), The Hague, Netherlands

Oct. 1962 – Jan. 1963: Director of Division Command Post (Cuban Crisis), 12th/15th Tactical Fighter Wings (MacDill AFB, FL)

12th Tactical Fighter Wing

15th Tactical Fighter Wing

Feb. 1963 – July 1966: Squadron Operations Officer, Squadron Commander, 4454th Combat Crew Training Wing (MacDill AFB, FL, and Davis-Monthan AFB, AZ)

4454th Combat Crew Training Wing

Aug. 1966 – Aug. 1967: Air War College (Maxwell AFB, AL)

Air War College

Sept. 1967 – Sept. 1968: Deputy Commander for Operations, 12th Tactical Fighter Wing (Cam Ranh Bay, Vietnam)

12th Tactical Fighter Wing

Oct. 1968 – Jan. 1970: Chief of Officer Assignments, Military Personnel Center (Randolph AFB, TX)

Air Force Personnel Center

March 1970 – Feb. 1971: Deputy Commander, then Commander of the 12th Tactical Fighter Wing (Phu Cat Air Base, Vietnam)

12th Tactical Fighter Wing

Apr. 1971 – Aug. 1972: Assistant Deputy Chief of Staff for Operations and Director of Safety, United States Air Forces, Europe (Ramstein AB, Federal Republic of Germany)

USAFE

Sept. 1972 – Jan. 1974: Chief of Staff, Military Assistance Group (Tehran, Iran)

Jan. 1974 – Sept. 1975: Deputy Chief of Staff for Operations, Tactical Air Warfare Center (Eglin AFB, FL)

Tactical Air Warfare Center

Sept. 1975 – Oct. 1976: Chief of Staff for Operations, Tactical Air Warfare Center (Eglin AFB, FL)

APPENDIX III
Decorations and Service Awards

1 Air Force Cross

1 Distinguished Service Cross

1 Silver Star

3 Legion of Merits

1 Distinguished Flying Crosses

1 Bronze Star

1 Meritorious Service Medal

41 Air Medals

1 Air Force Commendation Medal

1 Army Commendation Medal

4 Presidential Unit Citations

7 Outstanding Unit Awards

3 'V' Devices to Outstanding Unit Award

1 Air Force Organizational Excellence Award

1 Combat Readiness Award

1 Good Combat Medal

1 American Campaign Medal

1 Asiatic Pacific Campaign Medal

4 Bronze Battle Stars to Asiatic Pacific Medal

1 World War II Victory Medal

1 Army of Occupation Medal

2 National Defense Service Medals

1 Korean Service Medal

7 Bronze Battle Stars to Korean Service Medal
2 Armed Forces Expeditionary Medals
1 Vietnam Service Medal
6 Bronze Stars to Vietnam Medal
1 Air Force Longevity Award
6 Oak Leaf Clusters to Longevity Award
1 Armed Forces Reserve Medal
1 Small Arms Expert Marksman Award
1 Philippine Liberation Ribbon
2 Bronze Stars to Philippine Liberation Ribbon
1 Philippine Independence Ribbon
1 Vietnam Cross of Gallantry with Silver Star Medal
2 Vietnam Medal of Honor 1st Class
1 Republic of Vietnam Gallantry Cross with Palm
3 Korean Presidential Unit Citations
1 United Nations Service Ribbon
1 Republic of Vietnam Campaign

Bibliography

"A WWII Screamin Demon of the 7th FS." N/A. *www.demons7th.com/ACE.html.* Document. 27 August 2013.

"Armistice Agreement for the Restoration of the South Korean State (1953)." 10 July 2013. *www.ourdocuments.gov.* Document. 3 September 2013.

"Battle of Pusan Perimeter." n.d. *http://en.wikipedia.org/wiki/Battle_of_Pusan_Perimeter.* Document. 11 July 2013.

Bayat, Asef. *Life as Politics: How Ordinary People Change the Middle East, Second Edition.* Stanford, CA: Stanford University Press, 2010, 2013. Book.

Bible Gateway. 26 August 2013. Web Site. 26 August 2013. <http://www.biblegateway.com/verse/en/Matthew%207:12>.

Boyne, Walter J., Editor. *Air Warfare: An International Encyclopedia, Vol. 1.* ABC-Clio, 2002. Book.

Buljung, Brianna. *From the foxhole: American newsmen and the reporting of World War II.* USA: International Social Science Review, 2011. Document.

Cerone, Lt. Col. Scott "Hummer". *558th Flying Training Squadron Commander, Former A-10 Pilot* Author. 25 August 2013. Document.

"Consolidated B-24D Liberator." 4 February 2011. *www.nationalmuseum.af.mil.* Document. 26 August 2013.

Cooling, Franklin. *Case Studies in the Achievement of Air Superiority.* DIANE Publishing, 1994. Print.

"Cuban Missile Crisis." n.d. *www.nationalmuseum.af.mil/factsheets.* Document. 9 October 2013.

"Curtiss AT-9 Jeep/Fledgling." 4 Feb 2011. *www.nationalmuseum.af.mil.* Document. 15 July 2013.

Edwards, Paul. *Unusual Footnotes to the Korean War.* Long Island City, NY: Osprey Publishing, 2013. Book.

"F-86 Sabre vs. MiG-15 Armament." 7 June 2010. *www.nationalmuseum.af.mil.* Document. 15 July 2013.

"Leading Jet Ace: Capt. Joseph McConnell, Jr." 7 July 2010. *www.nationalmuseum.af.mil.* Document. 13 July 2013.

"Lindbergh's Transatlantic Flight: New York to Paris Timeline." 2007. *charleslindbergh.com.* Document. 27 August 2013.

"Lockheed P-38L Lightning." 4 February 2011. *www.nationalmuseum.af.mil.* Document. 15 July 2013.

"Maj. Gen. Claire Chennault." 18 August 2009. *www.nationalmuseum.af.mil.* Document. 26 August 2013.

Malayney, Norman. *12th Tactical Fighter Wing Assn., Historian* Author. 26 October 2013.

Mannion, Dennis. *Marine Cpl on ground during Siege of Khe Sanh, 1968* Author. 24 October 2013.

"Master Fighter Tactician: Frederick "Boots" Blesse." 8 June 2010. *www.nationalmuseum.af.mil.* Document. 18 July 2013.

"McDonnell Douglas F-4C Phantom II." 15 February 2011. *www.nationalmuseum.af.mil.* Document. 15 July 2013.

McManus, Tom. *Col. Parr's F-4 backseater Khe Sanh Mission* Author. 22 October 2013.

"Mitsubishi A6M2 Zero Factsheet." 4 February 2011. *www.nationalmuseum.af.mil.* Document. 15 July 2013.

Napalm. 25 August 2013. website. 25 August 2013. <www.u-s-hhistory.com/pages/h1859.html>.

Ortensie, R. Ray. *From the Pilot Factory, 1942.* College Station: Texas A&M University Press, 2005. Book.

Parr, Ralph S. *Personal Interview* Author. 22 December 2011.

Parr, Ralph S. *Personal Interview* Author. 30 November 2011.

Parr, Ralph S. *Personal Interview* Author. 12 January 2012. Interview.

Parr, Ralph S. *Personal Interview* Author. 23 December 2011. Interview.

Parr, Ralph S. *Personal Interview* Author. 13 January 2012. Interview.

Parr, Ralph S. *Personal Interview* Author. 24 January 2012. Interview.

Parr, Ralph S. *Personal Interview* Author. 9 February 2012. Interview.

Parr, Ralph S. *Personal Interview* Author. 29 February 2012. Interview.

Parr, Ralph S. *Personal Interview* Author. 1 March 2012. Interview.

Parr, Ralph S. *Personal Interview* Author. 2 March 2012. Interview.

Parr, Ralph S. *Personal Interview* Author. 21 March 2012. Interview.

Parr, Ralph S. *Personal Interview* Author. 23 March 2012. Interview.

Parr, Ralph S. *Personal Interview* Author. 17 April 2012. Interview.

Parr, Ralph S. *Personal Interview* Author. 19 April 2012. Interview.

Parr, Ralph S. *Personal Interview* Author. 20 April 2012. Interview.

Parr, Ralph S. *Personal Interview* Author. 16 May 2012. Interview.

Parr, Ralph S. *Personal Interview* Author. 18 May 2012. Interview.

Parr, Ralph S. *Personal Interview* Author. 6 June 2012. Interview.

Parr, Ralph S. *Personal Interview* Author. 5 June 2012. Interview.

Parr, Ralph S. *Personal Interview* Author. 8 June 2012. Interview.

Parr, Ralph S. *Personal Interview* Author. 27 June 2012. Interview.

Parr, Ralph S. *Personal Interview* Author. 29 June 2012. Interview.

Parr, Ralph S. *Personal Interview* Author. 11 July 2012. Interview.

Parr, Ralph S. *Personal Interview* Author. 13 July 2012. Interview.

Parr, Ralph S. *Personal Interview* Author. 1 August 2012. Interview.

Parr, Ralph S. *Personal Interview* Author. 3 August 2012. Interview.

Parr, Ralph S. *Personal Interview* Author. 22 August 2012. Interview.

Parr, Ralph S. *Personal Interview* Author. 24 August 2012. Interview.

Parr, Ralph S. *Personal Interview* Author. 29 August 2012. Interview.

Parr, Ralph S. *Personal Interview* Author. 31 August 2012. Interview.

Parr, Ralph S. *Personal Interview* Author. 7 September 2012. Interview.

Parr, Ralph S. *Personal Interview* Author. 9 Oct 2012. Interview.

Parr, Ralph S. *Personal Interview* Author. 10 October 2012. Interview.

Parr, Ralph S. *Personal Interview* Author. 1 November 2012. Interview.

Parr, Ralph S. *Personal Interview* Author. 2 November 2012. Interview.

Parr, Ralph S., Colonel, Commander, Phu Cat Air Base, Republic of Vietnam. "End of Tour Report." Annual Report with Lessons Learned. 1971. Document.

Pearson, Lt. Gen. Willard. *The War in the Northern Provinces, Vietnam Studies, 1966-1968.* Washington, D.C.: Department of the Army, 1975. Print.

Price, S.L. "The Second World War Kicks Off." 29 November 1999. *SI Vault.com.* Print. 10 August 2013.

<http://sportsillustrated.cnn.com/vault/article/magazine/MAG1017830>.

"RFK still not in political race." *The Daily Banner, Greencastle, Indiana* (1968): 1. Newspaper.

Shulimson, Jack, Leonard A. Blasiol, Charles R. Smith, and David A. Dawson. *U.S. Marines in Vietnam - The Defining Year 1968*. Washington, D.C.: History and Museums Division, Headquarters, U.S. Marine Corps, 1997. Print.

"Soviet Pilots over MiG Alley." 7 June 2010. *www.nationalmuseum.af.mil.* Document. 15 August 2013.

Tart, Larry and Robert Keefe. *The Price of Vigilance: Attacks on American Surveillance Flights*. Ballantine Books; Reprint edition, July 30, 2002. Book.

"The Southeast Asia War: Vietnam, Laos and Cambodia." 20 January 2012. *www.nationalmuseum.af.mil.* Document. 20 September 2013.

Thompson, Warren E. "Korean War." Boyne, Walter J., Editor. *Air Warfare: An International Encyclopedia, Vol 1*. ABC-CLIO, Inc, 2002. 354. Document.

"Truman told Churchill only 1 A-bomb to be dropped." *Japan Policy & Politics* 13 August 2001. Document.

Varhola, Michael. *Fire and Ice: The Korean War, 1950-1953, Vol 1 of History at a Glance Series, 213*. Basic Books, 2000. Book.

Zampini, Diego and Stephen Sherman. "Russian Aces over Korea, Mikoyan-Gurevich MiG-15 Fagot Pilots." 27 January 2012.

http://acepilots.com/russian/rus_aces.html. Document. 1 September 2013.

Index

(

(FAC), 28, 197

.

.50 caliber machine guns, 92
.50 caliber rounds, 95
.50-caliber guns, 70

"

"Bird Dog", 28

1

122-mm rockets, 24
12th Flying Training Wing, 258
12th FTW, 258
12th Operations Group, 20
12th Tactical Fighter Wing (TFW), 185
12th TFW, 186, 190, 191, 196, 197

12th TFW at Phu Cat, 186, 191
14.5 mm anti-aircraft guns, 36
1980 U.S. Olympic hockey team, 141
1st American Volunteer Group (AVG), 79
1st Marine Division, 89

2

20 mm cannon, 70, 196
20 mm external cannon, 37
22nd Air Refueling Wing, 113
23mm and one 37mm cannon, 105

3

304th North Vietnamese Division, 25
320th Division, 26

325C North Vietnamese Army Division, 25

335th Fighter-Interceptor Commander, 122

335th Fighter-Interceptor Squadron, 120, 121

335th FIS, 110

33rd Fighter Group, 83

388th Tactical Fighter Wing at Korat, KTAFB, Thailand, 249

389th and 480th Tactical Fighter Squadrons, 191

39th FIS, 110

4

49th Fighter Wing, 88, 89, 294

49th Group, 67

4th Fighter Wing, 115, 123, 176

4th Fighter-Interceptor Wing, 114, 120, 121, 123, 265, 266, 267, 268, 275, 277, 279, 281, 283, 295, 296

7

7 AF Commander, 188

7AF leadership, 233

7th Fighter Squadron, 67, 295

7th Squadron, 67, 89

8

82-mm mortar, 24

83rd IAK, 167

8th Tactical Fighter Wing, 249

A

A6M, 70

AAA, 31, 202

Abner, Alan K., 172

ADAMS, DONALD, 183

ADI, 201

Admiral Bland, 49

Advanced Training, 57

Aeroflot Il-12 *Coach. See* IL-12

Air Force Academy, 53

Air Force Association, 251

Air Force Cross, 17, 229, 257, 263, 303

Air Force Officer Qualification Test (AFOQT), 40

Airpower's Blacksmiths, 256

air-to-air, 14, 22, 64, 65, 93, 95, 108, 114, 120, 121, 130, 131, 135, 152, 154, 155, 187

air-to-ground, 22, 90, 92, 93, 95, 103, 120, 187, 198
Al Lopez Stadium, 221
Aleksandrov, 110
altimeter, 160, 201
American Embassy, 211
AMVETS, 251
Anderson, Maj. Rudolf Jr., 218
Andrews AFB, 76, 80
Antioch, California, 120
Apollo, 116, 185
Aptitude Test, 52
Arab-Israeli 6-Day War, 185
Armament Development and Test Center r, 222
Armistice, 121, 163, 164, 170, 176, 177, 178, 179, 180
Army, 24, 25, 27, 28, 35, 43, 48, 51, 52, 58, 79, 86, 92, 97, 102, 168, 178, 195, 211, 254, 259, 271, 284, 303
Army Air Corps, 43, 48, 52, 58, 79, 254, 259
Army and Navy Air Corps, 51
Artillery Forward Observer, 34
assassination, 221

asylum, 171
AT-9, 57
Atlantic, 45, 66
Auger Inn, 155, 243, 244, 256, 257, 258
Austin, Texas, 233

B

B-24, 60, 61
B-26, 57
B-29, 116, 117, 118, 119
B-50, 118
B-52, 229
BALDWIN, ROBERT, 184
Battalion Commander, 38, 227
Battle of Midway, 70, 125
Baugh, Sammy, 49
BECKER, RICHARD, 184
Berne, Switzerland, 73
BETTINGER, STEPHEN, 184
Bettinger, Steve, 120
Binh Tay, 197, 198
Biseem-e Najafabad, 210
Black Tuesday, 116
Blesse, 106, 107, 132, 133, 245
BLESSE, FREDERICK, 183
Blesse, Frederick C. "Boots", 104

BLU-27, 196

Blytheville, Arkansas, 57

Boeing, 175

boom operator, 203

Brett, Devol, 245

BT-13, 56

Burma, 78

BUTTELMANN, HENRY, 183

C

C-124 Globe master, 120

C-130, 29, 233

C-46, 163

C-47, 66, 77, 78

C-54, 66, 86

California, 103, 104, 113, 120, 162, 165

Cam Ranh Bay, 20, 186, 187, 227, 241, 245, 263, 264, 299

Cambodia, 190, 195, 197, 199, 234

Camp Stone man, 120

Cape Cod, 260, 294

Captain HX. Fenn, 49

Casner, A. James, 51

CBU, 205

Central Intelligence Agency (CIA), 208

Chaffee, Roger, 185

Chaucer, Geoffrey, 216

Chennault, Claire Lee, 78

Chiang Kai-shek, 79, 259

Chief of Staff, 211, 222, 271, 273, 300, 301, 302

Chiefs, 121, 171

China, 42, 70, 78, 79, 111, 126, 159, 162, 165, 166, 168

Chinese burp gun, 98, 99, 100

Chosen Retreat, 98

Chunggang-jin, 163

Churchill, 73, 175

Churchill, British Prime Minister Winston, 72

Clark, Gen. Mark, 169

Clark, Richard, 257

Coast Guard, 52

Col. Garrison. *See* Garrison, Col. Vermont

Col. Robin Olds, 22

Cold War, 20, 104, 142

Colliers, 169

Collins, Tom, 175

Colonel James Jabara Airport, 246

Combat Dining In, 257

Communists, 176

contact, 28, 30, 31, 36, 74, 189, 196, 199, 203

Court Martial, 82

Cox, 2nd Lt. Al, 125, 127, 137, 139, 245

Craigwell, Lt. Col. Ernest, 32, 230
CREIGHTON, RICHARD, 184
Cuba, 217, 218
Cuban Missile Crisis, 218
CURTIN, CLYDE, 184

D

Dak Pek, 196
Dak Seang, 196
Dallas, 221
Dandelions, 251
Dash one, 85
David, 141, 142, 172
DAVIS, GEORGE JR., 183
DeHaven, 67, 68
DeHaven, Bob, 67
Democratic Republic of Korea, 160
Der Gabelschwanz Teufel, 62
Desert Storm, 242
desk jockey, 186
DFC (Distinguished Flying Cross), 228
Dien Bien Phu, 26
Director of Safety, 210, 300
dirty guns, 140
Distinguished Flying Cross, 228, 275, 276, 278, 280, 282, 284, 286, 288, 290, 292
Distinguished Service Cross, 17, 265, 303
Dixon, Col. Robert J., 125
Dixon, Robert J., 245
DNIF, 152
dogfight, 1, 132, 137, 138, 140, 146, 150, 169, 268
Double Ace, 16, 112, 158, 256, 257
Drug Abuse, 206
DuPont, 175

E

Eagleston, Glenn T., 87
Edwards AFB, 60, 112
Eglin AFB, 301, 302
Eisenhower, Dwight D., 175
engagement, 96, 107, 130, 136, 150, 151, 152, 153, 163, 164, 194, 230
European theatre, 66
Everett, Pete "Speedy", 217

F

F-22 Raptors, 239
F-35 Lightning, 239
F-4, 34, 38, 187, 190, 193, 199, 202, 204, 217, 218, 230, 234, 239, 262
F-4C. *See* F-4C Phantom II

F-4C Phantom II, 21

F-80, 86, 88, 90, 92, 93, 95, 96, 103, 120

F-82, 87

F-84C, 84, 260

F-84F, 84

F-86, 15, 103, 104, 105, 107, 108, 109, 113, 114, 115, 118, 119, 124, 125, 127, 128, 131, 134, 139, 140, 143, 147, 167, 169, 170, 174, 238, 245, 247, 256, 265, 267, 276, 278, 280, 282

F-86 Sabre, 103, 119, 167, 256

F-86E, 109, 110, 112, 123

FAC, 28, 29, 30, 31, 32, 35, 38, 97, 98, 101, 102, 197, 199, 226, 230, 241

Fairchild PT-23, 54

Far East, 76, 86, 87, 89, 153, 173, 266, 268

Federal Archives Office, 73

Fedorets, 109, 110, 111, 112

Feltman, Tom, 174

FERNANDEZ, MANUEL JR., 183

Fifth Air Force, 151, 163

Fighting Eagles, 121

FISCHER, HAROLD, 183

Fishhook, 197

Florida, 216, 221, 222, 273

Flying Tigers, 70, 78, 79, 259

Form 5, 89

Fort Sam Houston National Cemetery, 254

Forward Air Controller, 28, 97

FOSTER, CECIL, 183

G

GABRESKI, FRANCIS, 183

Garrison, Col. Vermont, 122, 142

General Dynamics, 175

General Motors, 176

George AFB, 103, 104, 295

George Marshall, 50

GIBSON, RALPH, 184

Glinany, Capt. Dmitry, 167

Golden Gate Bridge, 27

Golden Star of the Heroes of the Soviet Union, 173

Goliath, 141, 142

Gosport tubes, 54

Great Depression, 42

Greatest Generation, 258

Green Bay Packers, 186

Green, Norman E., 110

Griffith Stadium, 49, 50

Grissom, Gus, 185

Group Commander, 60, 82, 185, 188

Group Director of Operations (DO), 188

Gruen, Victor, 209

H

H-19 rescue helicopter, 111

HAGERSTROM, JAMES, 183

Hall, Bill, 80, 81, 259, 260

Harrison, Lt. Gen. William K. Jr., 178

Hawaii, 49

Headquarters United States Air Forces Europe (USAFE), 210

Hill 861, 24, 34

Hill 881 North, 25

Hiroshima, 73, 74

Hitachi, 69

Hi-Vars, 92

Hokkaido Air Base, 80

Holy Moses, 113

Horner, General Chuck, 242

House of Commons, 175

Hymoff, Edward, 172

I

I Corps, 23

I, II, and III Corps, 190

IL-12, 158, 159, 160, 162, 163, 164, 165, 166, 167, 180, 248

Inchon Harbor, 86

Islamic, 209

J

J-79 engines, 22

JABARA, JAMES, 183

Jabara, Jimmy, 177, 245, 246

Javadieh, 210

Johnson, Col. James K., 121, 123

Johnson, Col. Scrappy, 249

JOHNSON, JAMES, 183

Johnson, James K., 177, 245

Johnson, Jimmy, 123, 150, 151

JOLLEY, CLIFFORD, 183

JONES, GEORGE, 183

K

K-2 airfield, 91

Kanggye, 126, 164, 166

KASLER, JAMES, 183

KC-135s, 202

Kennedy Administration, 218

Kennedy, President, 218, 221

Kennedy, President John F., 218

Khe Sanh, 23, 24, 26, 28, 29, 35, 37, 229, 230, 233, 253, 263

Khnadyan, 159

Khrushchev, Nikita, 218

Kimpo AB, 120

Kimpo Air Base, 87, 295

Kimpo Airfield (K-14), 176

KINCHELOE, IVEN JR., 184

Kon So-Sung, Lieutenant, 176

Korean War, 16, 20, 47, 84, 86, 88, 97, 104, 106, 108, 109, 116, 118, 122, 123, 124, 134, 153, 158, 162, 167, 168, 171, 174, 176, 178, 180, 182, 183, 185, 245, 256, 265, 267, 276, 278, 280, 282

Korean War (1950-1953), 20

Kum-Sok, 174

Kunueri, 98, 102

L

L-19 \Bird Dog, 28

Lake Placid, NY, 142

Laos, 25, 26, 190, 195, 197, 198, 199, 234

Las Vegas, Nevada, 250

LATSHAW, ROBERT JR., 184

Le Bourget Aerodrome, 75

leaflets, 173

Legion of Merit, 269, 271, 273

LILLEY, LEONARD, 183

LIMFACS (limiting factors), 195

Lincoln, Abraham, 180

Linda, 233, 234, 244

Lindbergh. *See* Lindbergh, Charles

Lindbergh, Charles, 75, 76, 78

Lingayen Gulf, 67

Lockheed Martin, 176

Lomphat, 198

London, England, 42

Long Island, New York, 75

Los Angeles, 62, 104, 113, 209

Love, Captain Ronald, 27

LOVE, ROBERT, 183

LOW, JAMES, 183

Lyndon B. Johnson, 19

M

M-3 .50-caliber machine-guns, 104

MacArthur, General, 241

MacArthur, General Douglas, 89, 254

MacDill, 216, 218, 219, 221, 239, 269, 297, 298

Manchuria, 105, 169

Manila, 41, 42, 43, 66

Mannion, Cpl. Dennis, 34

Margaret, 213, 214, 216, 222, 223, 238, 243, 244

MARSHAL, WINTON, 183

Maryland, 43

Massachusetts, 43, 87

Maxwell Field, 54

May Morrison Parr, 40

McConnell, 108, 109, 110, 111, 112, *See* McConnell, Joseph, Jr.

MCCONNELL, JOSEPH JR., 183

McConnell, Joseph, Jr., 108

McDonnell Douglas, 22, 239

McGill, 'Mac', 117

McManus, 27, 29, 36, 227, 235, 245

Medal of Honor, 228, 229, 253, 304

Medically Retired, 222

Mercury, 116

MIA, 112, 250

Miami Beach, Florida, 53

MiG Alley, 16, 105, 115, 119, 125, 126, 127, 142, 168

MiG-15, 16, 93, 105, 108, 109, 110, 112, 115, 117, 119, 131, 136, 168, 169, 171, 172, 174, 175, 181, 277, 278, 282

MiG-15bis *Fagot* '93', 109

Military Air Advisory Group (MAAG), 211

Miracle on Ice, 141

Mitsubishi, Nakajima, 69

MK-82, 196

Mojave, 113

MOORE, LONNIE, 183

MOORE, ROBERT, 184

Mosadeq, Mohammed, 208

Moscow, 159

Motobu Airfield, 70

Muroc AFB, California, 60

N

Nagasaki, 72, 73, 74

Nam Il, Gen., 178

Namsi airfield, 116

Napalm, 19, 23, 34, 35, 37, 84, 92, 196

Napalm (naphthenic politic acid), 34

National Anthem, 252

Naval Supply Corps, 52

Navy F-4Bs, 217
Navy F-8F, 81, 82
Navy Pontoon Aircraft, 41
Naziabad, 210
Nellis AFB, 131, 132
New Braunfels, 243, 254
New Braunfels, TX, 243, 254
New Mexico, 186
New York Times, 159
Nichols, Captain David, 172
Niemann, Robert, 112
No Guts No Glory, 132
Norfolk, 41
North African campaign, 62
North Korean air force, 86
North Vietnamese 68th and 164th Artillery Regiments, 26
North Vietnamese Army (NVA), 28, 35
Northrop-Grumman, 176
Norwegian freighter, 86
NVA, 23, 28, 35, 37, 198, 230

O

Oakland Raiders, 186
O'Brien, Pat, 50
OFAS, 244, 245
Officer Training School, 53

Okinawa, 70, 72, 74, 75, 76, 77, 293
Olds, Col. Robin, 249
Olympics, 142
Ontario, California, 62
Operation *Moolah*, 171, 172
Operations Officer, 204, 293, 295, 296, 297, 298
Otis AFB, 87
Otis Field, 260
OVERTON, DOLPHIN III, 184

P

P-38, 57, 62, 63, 64, 67, 68, 69, 70, 74, 80, 88, 238, 240, 293
P-38L model, 63
P-47, 69
P-47s, 80, 81, 113, 259
P-51, 69, 80, 239
P-51s, 80, 83, 85, 106, 113, 245, 259, 260
Pacific, 61, 62, 66, 69, 87, 120, 125, 303
Pacific theatre, 66
Pamela, 243
Panama, 260
Panmunjom, 124, 178
Paris, France, 75
Parr O'Club, 243, 258
Parr, May Morrison, 40

PARR, RALPH JR., 183

Pasqualicchio, Pancho, 245

Pasqualicchio, Robert P., 80

Paul, 244

Pearl Harbor, 49, 62, 79, 254

Pentagon, 83, 116, 117, 119, 185, 210, 218, 259

People's Liberation Army Air Force (PLAAF), 168

Pepelyayeu, Colonel Yevgeni, 173

Petitpierre, Max, 73

Phantom, 21, 29, 30, 31, 227, 262

Philadelphia, 49

Philadelphia Eagles, 49

Philippine invasion, 67

Philippines, 41, 42, 43, 49, 66, 67, 293

Phu Cat, 186, 190, 191, 192, 194, 205, 206, 238, 244, 300

Pickett, Col. Larry, 249

Pickrel, Ed, 244

pierced steel planking (PSP), 91

piper, 155

pipper, 64, 145, 146, 147

Ploesti, Rumania, 61

police action, 96

political upheaval, 19

Portsmouth, Virginia, 40

Potsdam Conference, 73

Potsdam, Germany, 72

Prisoners of War (POW), 250

PT-23, 55

Pusan, 88, 89

Pusan Perimeter, Battle of, 88

Pyle, Ernie, 71, 72

R

R and R, 95

Ralph Parr Pack, 249

Ralph S. III, 243

Randolph AFB, 191, 218, 238, 244, 255, 256, 257, 299

Randolph Officer's Club, 243, 258

Rated Officer Assignments, 191

RB-50, 159

Red River Valley Fighter Pilot Association, 249

Red Stripe, 140

remotely piloted aircraft, 240

Replacement Training Unit (RTU), 200

Republic of Vietnam (RVN), 206

RF-101s, 218

RFK, 19

Ricker, 1st Lt. Mervin, 125

RISNER, ROBINSON, 183

River Rats, 250

Roberts, John, 153, 155, 245

Rocketeers, 121

Roosevelt Field, 75

Roosevelt, President, 71, 79

Roosevelt, President Franklin, 79

Roswell, New Mexico, 76, 83, 260

ROTC, 53

Routes 92 and 9, 26

Rowe, Kenneth, 175

RUDDELL, GEORGE, 183

Russia, 45, 141

S

SAC, 260

Safety Officer, 204

San Antonio, Texas, 218

San Francisco, 27, 253

Saturday Evening Post, 172

Scatback, 189

Schirra, Walter, 116

Schwarzkopf, General, 242

Scotland, 47, 230

Semenov, 112

Sen. Eugene J. McCarthy, 19

Sen. Robert F. Kennedy, 19

Seoul, 86, 118, 176, 198

Shahbaz Jonoubi, 210

Sheryl, 244

Shorin, 110

Siege of Khe Sanh, 19

Silver Star, 267, 303, 304

Silver, Major Edward D., 32, 230

Sino-Soviet border, 159

Sinuiju, 116, 117, 126, 173

situational awareness, 68, 154, 194, 213, 239

South Korea, 86, 173, 176, 178, 294

Southeast Asia (SEA), 191

Soviet Union, 159, 160, 166, 168, 171, 173

Spartanburg, South Carolina, 53

Special Forces Camps, 196

Spirit of St. Louis, 75

Stalin, Soviet leader Joseph, 73

State Department, 166

stick and rudder artist, 261

Stoeng Treng, 198

Student Defense Service Committee, 51

Sunchon, 117

Super Bowl, 186

T

T-33, 90

Tactics Evaluation shop (Stan/Eval), 192

Taegu, 91, 294

Taj Mahal, 258

Tampa, Florida, 221

Tehran, 209, 210, 211, 301

Tennessee, 243

The Golden Rule, 40

The Need To Belong, 248

Thompson sub-machine guns, 213

Thunderbird, 241

THYNG, HARRISON, 184

Toan Thang, 197, 198

Toboggan, 203

Tokyo, 241

Top Gun, 132

Towed target, 65

troops in contact (TIC), 28, 199

Truman, President Harry, 72, 86

Tu-2 bombers, 119

Type-A, 40

typhoon of the century, 71

U

U-2s, 218, 260

Ubon AFB, Thailand, 249

UHF transmissions, 202

United Nations, 88, 124, 169, 171, 172, 173, 178, 179, 265, 267, 276, 278, 280, 282, 304

University of Delaware, 175

University of North Dakota, 175

USSR, 168

V

Vandenberg, General, 116

VFW, 251

Viet Cong, 196, 198

Vladivostok, Russia, 45

Voice of the United Nations, 173

W

Walnut Ridge, Arkansas, 55

Washington Daily News, 71

Washington Redskins, 49

Washington, D.C., 49, 50, 53, 76, 259, 293

WESCOTT, WILLIAM, 184

WHISNER, WILLIAM JR., 183

White, Edward, 185

Wichita, Kansas, 246, 249

Wichita, KS, 113

Wills, James, 112

Wing Tactics Evaluations Officer, 204
Wofford College, 53
Wonsan harbor, 117
World War II ace, 22
Worldwide Gunnery Championship, 106
WSO, 22, 189
WWI, 45, 47
WWII, 22, 41, 45, 51, 58, 62, 71, 78, 79, 80, 87, 88, 125, 178, 198, 240, 254, 259
WWII B-17, 22

Y

Yalu. *See* Yalu River
Yalu River, 105, 115, 126, 127, 139, 147, 158, 163, 164, 169, 170, 267, 276
Yeager, Chuck, 175, 260
Yefremov, 110
Yellow Sea, 109, 117, 126

Z

Zero, Japanese, 69, 70